Creating *the* VINTAGE *look*

Creating *the* VINTAGE *look*

35 WAYS TO UPCYCLE FOR A STYLISH HOME

Ellie Laycock

CICO BOOKS
LONDON NEW YORK

To Dave and Denise for your unswerving support and to Malakai, for the inspiration. Dedicated to the memory of my dear friend and mentor, Claire Richardson... I think of you every day.

This edition published in 2018 by CICO Books
An imprint of Ryland Peters & Small

341 E 116th St,
New York, NY 10029

20–21 Jockey's Fields,
London, WC1R 4BW

www.rylandpeters.com

10 9 8 7 6 5 4 3 2 1

First published in 2013 by CICO Books

A CIP catalog record for this book is available from the Library of Congress and the British Library.

ISBN: 978-1-78249-568-0

Printed in China

EDITOR: Katie Hardwicke
DESIGNER: Vicky Rankin
ILLUSTRATOR: Harriet de Winton
PHOTOGRAPHER: Claire Richardson
STYLIST: Nel Haynes and Ellie Laycock

Contents

Introduction

I've loved rummaging around hunting for treasures since I was very young, so much so, I've made a business out of it. Of course, everybody's version of "treasure" is different. To the five-year-old me it was finding a tiny junk jewelry lizard with green stone eyes and a missing leg in the bottom of an old shoe box. To Winston Smith in George Orwell's 1984, it was his junk store find of a blank vintage diary in a world with no free speech. The point is that vintage items are special because they are intrinsically imbued with a history and a story.

Upcycling is not a new phenomenon, though the word might be relatively new. Re-cycling means to use something, break it down, remake, and use again. Upcycling means to re-use something (without breaking it down) for a new purpose. We've probably all done some without even realizing it and previous generations certainly have. Ever used an old mug as a pen pot? A shell as a soap dish? This book is about finding vintage items that speak to you and looking for ways to turn them into your own personal treasures for your home. That is, after all, where the heart is.

USEFUL TOOLS AND EQUIPMENT

Before you embark on your upcycled projects make sure you have the right tools and equipment to hand. Some projects require special tools or materials and these will be listed in the "You will need" list. Here are a few items that you will find useful for most general purposes:

GLUES AND TAPES

All-purpose glue

Hot glue gun

PVA glue

Spray mount adhesive

Double-sided tape

Masking tape

SEWING KIT

Sewing machine

Needles and thread

Tapestry needles and yarn

Pins and safety pins

Stitch ripper

Iron

Fabric scissors

MEASURING AND MARKING TOOLS

Tape measure/ruler

Marker pens/pencils

WORKSHOP TOOLS

Paintbrushes (various sizes)

Pots/dishes for paint and glue

Plastic spatula

Hammer

Nails and panel pins

Drill and drill bits (including countersink and screwdriver bits)

Rawl plugs

Screws (various sizes)

Screwdrivers (flat head and cross head)

Safety goggles

Staple gun and staples

Sandpaper (various grades)

Sanding block

Wire wool

Craft knife/scalpel (including square blade)

Cutting mat

Handsaw for cutting wood

Hack saw for cutting metal or plastics

Jigsaw for cutting freehand curves

Spirit level

Tracing paper

Old newspapers/dust sheets

QUICK GUIDE TO PAINTS AND VARNISHES

Matt and gloss paints
Originally oil-based but due to recent innovations you can now buy water-based versions of these paints. Water-based paints dry more quickly, release fewer harmful fumes, and are kinder to the planet as you can wash brushes out in water rather than in chemicals. They are also safer for children's rooms.

Spray paint
Plasti-kote Projekt Paint is recommended as it is safe to use on children's items and is available in small amounts, and a variety of colors. Always use in a well-ventilated area, protect your work surface, and follow the instructions on the can.

Decorator's varnish
Can be used to seal, protect, and decorate a wide range of surfaces, is odor free, water-based (so low impact on the environment, safe for children, and easy tool cleaning), and forms a hard-wearing coating.

Invisible Bookshelf

Chapter 1 **Vintage Living Room**

Make your own unique decorative accessories, practical pieces, soft furnishings, and even furniture for your living spaces—from a stylish vintage tin clock (page 22) quirky jello mold tea light holders (page 34).

Vinyl Record Coasters

Musical Score Lampshade

Sometimes less is more. This is a simple project that shows you how to transform a plain lampshade into a subtly textured and personalized statement piece that will be truly unique and look fantastic with both the light on and off!

YOU WILL NEED

A pale plain drum lampshade

Vintage paper, such as sheet music or maps

All-purpose glue or double-sided sticky tape

Scissors

Fire retardant spray

1 Cut your paper into squares and rectangles in a variety of sizes—the printed lines on musical score sheets work well as cutting guidelines. Just cut a handful of pieces to start with so that you can play around with the design. You can cut more as and when you need them.

2 Start at the bottom of the shade. Hold a piece of paper up to the bottom of the shade and decide how much of it you want to hang down below the edge. Now apply glue or a strip of double-sided tape along the top of the paper and stick it to the shade.

3 Create a block approximately 5 pieces wide and work your way up to the row below the top of the shade, applying layers of paper pieces. Vary the size and shape to create a non-uniform and more interesting look. If you work upward, then each new piece you apply will cover and disguise the join of the piece below. Add some long strips occasionally to give it more texture and depth.

4 As an interesting detail, I not only made sure that all the pieces of paper that I stuck around the very top of the shade were lined up neatly with the edge of the shade itself, but I also selected pieces that had a line printed across (in this case the edge of the musical stave) to give a uniformity to the overall design.

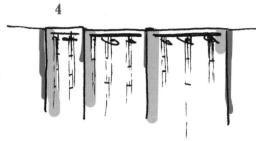

5 Continue working in blocks around the shade until you have covered it all. Step back from your work now and again to see how you are progressing. As your skill increases you may find that your technique changes slightly so stepping back for an overall view will help you keep the design even over the whole shade. You can always go back over it and add extra pieces here and there (or take them away!).

6 Finish by covering the paper pieces with a fire retardant spray for safety.

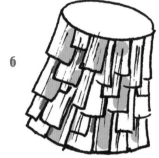

VARIATIONS

• For a neat bottom edge, simply trim the ends and glue to the edge.

• Use your favorite black and white photographs to decorate the shade instead—either photocopy them or scan and print multiple copies. You can use anything as long as it's not too thick so that the light can shine through.

• Rather than having loose ends, stick the whole piece flat to the shade and build up to make a patchwork design.

• Add a traditional shade trim around the top or base.

Tapestry Footstool

I never really understood the point of these little footstools, usually dark in color and slightly sad-looking. They were just the kind of thing you would trip over in Grandma's house. But, I have to say, I've started to warm to them now that I've realized their potential for a makeover. They are great for little ones to perch on or to put your feet up with a cuppa! Revamp them with kitsch tapestries that pick out colors from your décor or use scenes that make you smile, and you'll find you've made a little gem that sits well in any style of room.

YOU WILL NEED

Completed tapestries—you'll find these in frames, as pillow covers, or as abandoned projects in all kinds of junk stores, garage sales, and antique fairs

Footstool

Tapestry needle and tapestry yarn

Staple gun

Marker pen (optional)

1 Measure your footstool top and sides. The aim is to create a box shape from tapestry pieces that will fit snugly over your existing footstool with enough depth to fold under and staple to secure.

2 Now measure your tapestries and work out which bit you want to go where. I had a large tapestry that covered the top and short sides, so I just had to sew on 2 side panels. If you're working with small pieces, you will need to sew them together to create pieces large enough to cover the top and sides, remembering to add some extra to fold under. Use whip stitch and a tapestry needle and matching yarn to join the pieces.

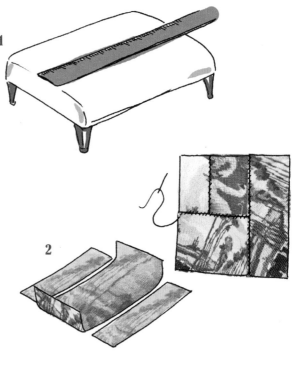

3 Create seams where you need to join the pieces to make a "box." Mark the seams on the reverse of the tapestry—I traced the line of stitches with a marker pen to make it easier to see where to stitch. It's fairly simple to sew in a straight line on a tapestry if you follow the line of needlework on the canvas. Remember, you're working on it inside out at this stage. Use whip stitch or, for a stronger seam, backstitch, taking a small seam allowance.

4 Once you have made your "box," turn it the right way out and place it over the footstool and make sure it fits.

5 With the tapestry in place, turn the stool upside down. Pull the middle of one edge taut, tuck under any excess, and staple to the underside of the frame (it will be out of sight once right way up) with one staple in the center. Do the same on the opposite side, pulling the tapestry taut—check that it looks OK on the top and isn't too loose or too taut and distorted. Then repeat with the remaining two sides, adding just one staple in the center of each side. This keeps the tapestry tension even. Once you are happy, add a couple more staples either side on each edge.

6 Tuck the tapestry back on itself around the legs and staple along the underside of the four sides. Don't staple to the legs as you might see the staples.

VARIATIONS

• Add trim around the edge for a more elaborate look or paint the legs to complement your tapestry designs.

• Use any type of textile that you like, from oversized chunky knits for a soft and quirky style to burlap (hessian) coffee sacks for an industrial look. You could even use leather from an old jacket you no longer wear—just follow the steps above and use glue instead of stitching to join the pieces.

Silk Scarf *Pillow*

Beautiful vintage scarves are often kept in pristine condition—perhaps you have a special one that you no longer wear hidden away in a drawer, or have been handed down a family favorite that you don't know what to do with? Here's how to turn it into a striking pillow that can work in almost any room of the house. Use bold, bright patterns for a shot of color on the sofa, delicate florals for the bedroom, or quirky retro prints for a kid's room.

Tip

For a pillow that looks nicely filled, always select a pillow form that is about 2in (5cm) larger than your cover. Common square pillow form sizes are 18in (45cm), 22in (55cm), and 26in (65cm), so for maximum plumpness make your cover 16in (40cm), 20in (50cm), or 24in (60cm) square.

YOU WILL NEED

Vintage silk scarf

Backing fabric

Scissors

Tape measure

Sewing machine and matching thread

Pillow form (pad)

1 Measure the scarf. Scarves can be quite large so use most or all of it to make a floor pillow or decide how much you want to trim off to make a smaller square pillow for the sofa.

2 Once you have decided on your size, cut down the scarf if necessary, allowing 2in (5cm) for the seam on all sides. So, to make a 22-in (56-cm) square cover, cut your piece to 26in (66cm) square. If the scarf has pin holes you may wish to trim them off, if it still leaves you with a large enough square for your desired pillow size. To really show off the scarf design, position it centrally. If it's a certain part of the design that you like then make that the center of your pillow.

3 Take your backing fabric and cut two pieces. Each piece should measure the full height of your scarf including seams and approximately three-quarters of the width. So, for the above example, cut pieces approximately 26 x 20in (66 x 50cm).

2

3

4 Lay the scarf on your work surface with the right side facing you. Lay one piece of backing fabric right side down over the scarf, lining up the left-hand edge, and pin in place. Fold the right-hand edge of the backing fabric back by approximately 2in (5cm) so that the right side is facing you. Pin in place at the top and bottom of the fold. To minimize fraying, confident sewers can run a zigzag or overlocking stitch along the raw edge of the fold.

4

5 Repeat for the other piece of backing fabric. Align it face down on the right-hand side of the scarf and pin. Take the left edge and fold it back by 2in (5cm) to the right and pin at the top and bottom edge.

5

6 Keeping everything nice and flat, machine stitch around all four edges, taking a 2in (5cm) seam. Stitch over the overlapping folds of the back pieces. Turn the cover right side out through the envelope back and insert your pillow form (pad). You have made your pillow cover!

6

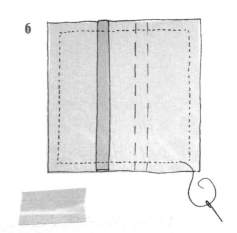

VARIATIONS

• Add a buttonhole halfway along the exterior fold for extra hold and decoration. Or, if you're feeling adventurous, you could add a pompom trim between the covers when sewing the four edges.

Vinyl Record Coasters

Vinyl records, now obsolete or the preserve of specialist collectors, have been victims of the relentless march of technology and the digital age. For quite a few of us, though, they still bring out a touch of nostalgia and I fondly remember the first vinyl 7-inch single that I bought with my pocket money one Saturday back in the day! Here are a few ideas of how to upcycle these historic discs into fun and quirky homewares.

YOU WILL NEED

For the coasters:

7-inch vinyl records (singles)

Square cork coasters, about 4 x 4in (10 x 10cm)

Ruler

Chinagraph pencil

All-purpose glue

Strong sharp pair of long-handled scissors

Sanding block with medium to fine grade sandpaper

For the placemats:

Colored vinyl records— 7-inch, 12-inch, or albums

Round cork placemats or trivets in a similar size to the records

All-purpose glue

1 Place your record down on a flat work surface with the side you want as the top of your coaster facing you. Make sure the label is straight. Place your cork coaster over the top and use the ruler to centre it. Measure from each coaster edge (in the center of one side) out to the widest point of the record and gently move the coaster around until this measurement is equal on all four sides.

2 Gently hold the coaster in place and draw round the edge with the chinagraph pencil or marker.

3 Using sharp scissors, cut along one side of your marked square, straight across the record and just slightly on the inside of your mark. Go carefully as you don't want the record to split. Repeat for all four sides. Take care, as the corners will be sharp.

4 With a sanding block, lightly sand across one of the corners. Work gently, following the edge of the record, to form a rounded corner. You can lightly sand the straight edge too if you wish, but take care not to scratch the top surface.

5 Clean away the dust from the sanding. Turn the record over and apply all-purpose glue to the back. If your record has perforations in it, keep the glue away from these areas, paying special attention to any raised areas. Bring the cork coaster and the record together, align, and push firmly together. You could leave an old telephone directory or catalog on top as they dry to keep the pressure applied. Repeat to make a set.

VARIATIONS

• If you can't find colored vinyl, you can spray paint a normal record. Mask off the label first to protect it.

• Make a cake stand by connecting different sized records with 2- or 3- tier cake stand parts, available from craft shops. Attach self-adhesive felt pads to the base of the cake stand for added stability.

• Use a 12-inch record instead of a tin and follow the steps for attaching hands from the Vintage Tin Clock project on page 22. You can add a hook on the back of the clock mechanism to hang your vinyl wall clock.

6 Use colored vinyl records for a brighter look. These look great as placemats—simply glue them to matching round cork mats or trivets.

Vintage Tin Clock

Old cookie or chocolate tins are often decorated with gorgeous designs and pictures and it seems such a shame to hide them away in the kitchen cabinets. With just a few tools and a clock mechanism, you can transform your tin into a vintage timepiece to grace your desk, mantelpiece, bookshelf, or even it hang on the wall.

YOU WILL NEED

Vintage tin

Marker pen and ruler

Drill and drill bit

Clock movement and battery—choose a mechanism with a short spindle

Pliers (preferably long-nose pliers)

1 Measure your tin lid and find and mark the center point. If your tin is rectangular, measure across the shortest side and make a note of this measurement. When selecting your clock mechanism, you will want the longest hand to measure **less** than this measurement so that once fixed in place, the hands will be able to sweep round without getting caught.

2 Select your mechanism. Mechanisms come in long, medium, or short spindle sizes and as the tin lid is quite thin you'll need the short spindle length. They also come in a variety of hand designs and colors, so select one that looks good with the tin you have chosen. I chose a gold one because my tin lid had gold accents and, because the design is quite elaborate, I opted for straight clock hands rather than ornate ones to stop it looking too fussy.

3 Your mechanism should come with instructions on what sized drill bit to use. I used a 5⁄16in (8mm) diameter HSS drill bit and drilled my hole in the center of the lid (see page 120). You could remove the lid from the tin to make this step easier.

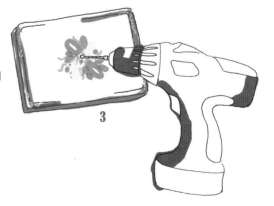

4 Now assemble the clock. Lay the mechanism on a flat surface with the spindle upward and remove the nut and washer. Gently push the movement through the back of the hole in your lid (leaving the rubber washer in place) and replace the brass washer and nut on the front. Tighten gently with pliers.

5 Now carefully take your "hour" hand and place it on the spindle with it pointing up to "12 o'clock;" it should push gently down into position. Next, take the "minute" hand and repeat this process, avoiding any twisting motion. The spindle is tiered so that the hands have some distance between them in order to turn without colliding so this hand won't go as far onto the spindle as the hour hand.

6 Lastly, gently place your "second" hand onto the pin in the center of the movement. View the clock from the side to check that the hands can turn freely (if you accidentally bend a hand, remove and gently sweep through your fingers to straighten).

7 Insert the battery into the mechanism box, set the correct time using the dial on the reverse of the mechanism, and clip your tin lid back onto your tin. Now you have a beautiful vintage tin clock to display.

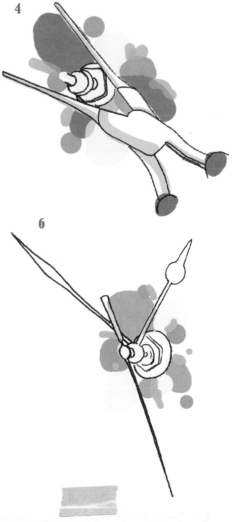

VARIATIONS

• Glue a picture hook to the back of the tin to hang on the wall.

• Use a plain tin and paint or decoupage numbers onto it in the correct positions to create a numbered clock face.

Stamp Collection *Placemats*

When having a sort out, I rediscovered my stamp collection from when I was a kid. There were so many brightly colored stamps with beautiful designs from all around the world, that I felt inspired to find a way to display them, and so created these colorful placemats. You can use any paper items, from collectable vintage tea cards to maps, sheet music, gift wrap, even concert tickets or copies of favorite photos. They'll certainly spark conversation over dinner!

YOU WILL NEED

Selection of stamps or paper items

Cork placemats

Large sheet of paper

Pencil

Glue to bond cork and plastic

Laminator (I had a copy store do it for me), or 2 sheets of sticky-backed plastic

Craft knife or scalpel

Scissors

Cutting mat

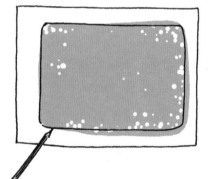

1 Lay your placemat on top of the sheet of paper and draw around it using the pencil to define the area to decorate.

1

2 Arrange your stamps in a pleasing pattern and begin to glue them onto the paper. You could arrange them by color or theme, whatever appeals. Don't worry if they go over the edge, as anything overlapping your pencil line will be trimmed off later.

2

3 Laminate the paper and stamps. Most large stationers or copy stores offer this service. You could use one sheet of clear sticky-backed plastic on each side and do it yourself but this will not be quite as sturdy or durable.

4 Trim off any excess laminate around the edge with scissors or a craft knife, leaving approximately ½in (1cm) extra outside of your guideline. Spread glue evenly across the back of your laminate and press it down onto the cork mat. Try to line up your guidelines with the edge of the mat. Let it dry—you could put some old heavy catalogs or directories on top to help apply pressure while it dries.

5 Once dry, place on a cutting mat and carefully trim away the excess laminate using a sharp knife or scalpel, taking care not to nick the cork base and making the edges as flush as possible.

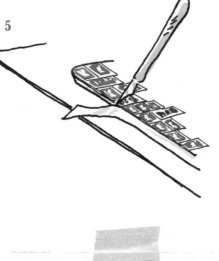

VARIATIONS

• Use colored or patterned paper underneath the stamps and let some show through in your design.

• This is a great way to update your existing placemats if they're looking worn or you want a completely new look. Follow the steps above, lightly sanding the surface first so that the glue will stick.

• For extra sturdiness, seal the edges with wax, clear lacquer, or varnish.

• Make some matching coasters!

Invisible Bookshelf

A good book is timeless and vintage hardbacks have a beautiful quality to them. Some, sadly, become obsolete along the way or succumb to age and "foxing," but these can be repurposed into a striking shelf that seemingly defies the laws of physics and will certainly become a talking point in any location. Just make sure you don't use a first edition!

YOU WILL NEED

A large hardback book

Sticky-back Velcro (male and female)

2 x L-shaped wall brackets (flat, not ridged)

Pencil

Spirit level

Drill, drill bit, rawl plugs, and screws (suitable for your wall)

1 Open the book at the back page and measure the back inside cover from top to bottom. Use a pencil to mark one-third down and two-thirds down.

1

2 Measure the width of the back inside cover. **Note:** It is important to make sure that the short ends of your wall brackets are the same size as this measurement (or smaller) so that they will fit.

3

3 Cut two strips of Velcro a fraction of an inch shorter than the width of your back page. Peel apart the male Velcro (bristly) from the female Velcro (soft loops). Remove the backing from one strip of male Velcro and stick it onto the inside back cover horizontally along the mark, one-third from the top. Repeat with the other strip of male Velcro along your second mark. Your pencil mark should be in the center of the strip.

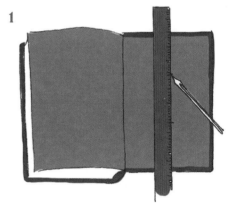

4 Make sure your brackets are free from dirt and grease. Place one bracket over the back page of the book with the end of the short side to the spine of the book, the bend of the bracket at the right-hand edge of the cover, and the long arm of the bracket pointing upward. Make a note of which part of the bracket is connecting with the Velcro on the book. This is where you'll need to stick the female Velcro. Peel away the backing from the female strips of Velcro and stick one onto the correct side of the short end of each bracket.

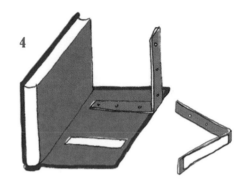

5 Now bring the two pieces of Velcro back together again by positioning the brackets over the strips in the book and pressing firmly together. Close the book. You have made the shelf!

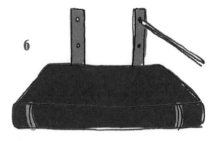

6 Hold the shelf up to the wall and, using a spirit level to make sure it's straight, mark in pencil where the holes are in your brackets. Drill holes and fix the brackets to the wall (see page 122). These brackets will be hidden once you add more books to your shelf and it will look like the books are floating by magic!

VARIATIONS

• Just use one centrally placed bracket if you are not going to add too many books to the shelf.

• Paint the book to match your wall color for an even subtler look.

• Cut a small recess in the pages at the front of the book for a super secret hiding place!

Mirror Side Table

Tired table, heavy old mirror. Apart they may seem like their best days are behind them but bring them together and you can create a beautiful and practical side table that, like all beautifully mirrored furniture, will hardly seem like it's there!

YOU WILL NEED

Round vintage mirror with wooden back

Round side table

Sandpaper

TSP or sugar soap

Primer

Wood paint and paintbrush

Masking tape (optional)

Hot glue gun

1 The key to this project is selecting a mirror that is at least the same diameter (or larger) than your side table (or selecting a table that is the same size or smaller than your mirror!). Lay your mirror face up on the table, center it, and check that it covers the table top. Vintage mirrors usually come with a flat wooden back, which is essential for the table top to be strong, especially if it extends out from your table base.

2 Give the side table a good sanding down and remove all dust and any dirt. TSP or sugar soap solution is good for this—follow the instructions on the packaging.

3 Apply one layer of primer to the table but leave the top surface unpainted. Make sure you avoid any drips in the finish. Let dry. Paint the table with one coat of paint in your chosen color, again leaving the table top unpainted and avoiding drips in the finish. You may need one or two coats depending on the color and type of paint you use.

4 If you wish to paint the wooden back of the mirror so that it matches your table legs, you can either mask off the glass with masking tape or you can remove the mirror and paint the wood. Work on a flat surface, like the floor, with an old blanket laid out to protect the delicate glass and carefully remove the mirror fixings. Prepare and paint your wood. Pay special attention to the edges of the frame, as this is the part that you will see. Reassemble when dry.

5 To assemble the table, place the mirror face down on an old blanket on the floor then place the table upside down onto the mirror back. Position it centrally and mark around the edge with a pencil. Remove the table, apply glue to the table top, and reposition the table using your pencil mark to guide you. Once aligned, press firmly. Remember, if you are using a hot glue gun that you need to work swiftly as the glue sets quickly!

6 Once dry, turn the table the right way up and give the glass a polish. Add a beautiful vase of flowers and you have a glamorous addition for any room.

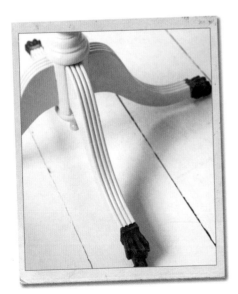

VARIATIONS

• Transform your mirror table top with tips from the "Mirror Makeover" project on page 68 to create a unique customized piece of furniture.

• Wrap colorful ribbons or strips of fabric around the table legs for a touch of homespun style.

• Mirror tables look great with candles or lamps on, as the reflective surface helps bounce the light around the room and can create interesting effects.

Jello Mold Tea Light Holder

Lighting is important for creating the right atmosphere and candlelight is a wonderful addition to any table where friends and family may gather, where it combines with the reflective elements of glass or metal to create beautiful, mood-enhancing effects. Use vintage metal kitchenalia, such as these cute little jello molds, to create a centerpiece for tea lights to twinkle in and guests to talk about.

YOU WILL NEED

6 small vintage tin jello molds

Hammer and large nail

Medium grade sandpaper

Piece of wood, preferably weathered or aged (as long and wide as you wish but at least ¾in/2cm thick)

Pencil

Tape measure or ruler

Screwdriver and 6 x wood screws (No 8 x ¾in/2cm)

Drill and small wood drill bit (size 2.5)

1 Turn a jello mold upside down and position a nail in the center of the base. Give it a firm tap with the hammer so that it pierces the base. Repeat for every jello mold.

2 Sand any rough edges on the base wood so that the surface will be smooth and safe to handle. When using old wood, make sure there are no nails sticking out. If there are, remove them with pliers or a claw hammer, or hammer them down flat—making sure they are not in the areas you wish to drill or screw into.

3 Space the jello molds evenly along the wood. Check your spacing with a tape measure or ruler. Once in place, mark through the holes in the bases with a pencil. Check that the molds are positioned centrally across the width of the wood, too, and if necessary redraw your marks at the midway point.

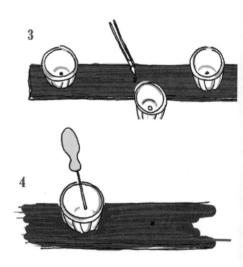

4 Use a thin drill bit for wood, such as size 2.5, and drill pilot holes into the wood where your marks are. Place the tip of a short wood screw through the hole in the mold and align with the pilot hole in the wood. Screw down to secure the mold. If your mold bent inward slightly when you hammered the original hole into it, screwing it down here will correct it.

5 Add tea lights, transport your lighting to its ideal location, and enjoy!

Crochet Vases

Crocheted doilies are a common find when hunting for vintage textiles. Hours of fine needlework goes into making them so it seems fitting to show it off around a beautiful glass vase as a centerpiece. Create your own unique designs using clear glass vases as a base and vintage doilies or lacework for an ornate surface pattern. Here, I'll show you two different ways to achieve this look.

YOU WILL NEED

Vintage doilies, crochet, or lacework

Clear glass vase: straight-sided for Method 1; over-hanging tops for Method 2

Crystal drops or beads (optional)

Sewing needle and thread

PVA glue

Decorator's varnish

Paintbrush

Craft knife

> **Tip**
> If the crochet or lace pattern dictates where to cut, cut too short rather than too long and have some clear glass exposed at the top and bottom of the vase.

Method 1: Crochet Sleeve

1 Lay your crochet piece out flat, right side down, on a clean, dry work surface. Lay your glass vase on its side on top of the crochet. Align the top of the crochet with the top of the vase. Cut a straight line across the length of the crochet, in line with where it meets the bottom of the vase.

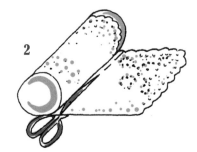

2 Hold the left-hand side of the crochet work to the side of the vase, roll the vase to the right taking the crochet with it, until it goes all the way around the vase and meets the fabric again. Cut along this line from top to bottom in a straight line. Wrap around the vase to check that it is a snug fit and not too loose—if it seems shy you can add tension when you sew it together but if it's too loose it will sag, so trim a fraction more off.

3 Attach your sewing thread to the bottom corner of the crochet. With the crochet wrapped round the vase, start to sew the two edges together with running stitch. Work your way up the side of the vase until you reach the top. If your crochet has large holes, run the thread through the pattern to hide it in between the seam.

4 Brush PVA glue onto the vase, through the crochet, to coat it with a generous layer of glue. Take the time to work the PVA well into the crochet with a stippling motion. If any edges are lifting, paint PVA between the crochet and the glass and stick down. The layer of glue may appear to be thick but it will soak into the crochet as it dries. Wait for this layer to dry.

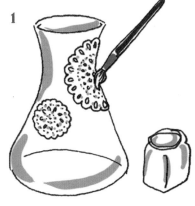

5 Coat the vase with a generous layer of decorator's varnish to create a waterproof seal. Let dry. Remove any PVA glue and varnish from areas of exposed glass. It should pick away easily or you can use a small craft knife to lift the edges and peel away. Do this for as many "holes" as you wish.

Method 2: Dotty Doily

1 Gather some circular doilies and/or cut round shapes from other pieces. Take your largest doily and decide where to place it on the vase. Paint this area with PVA glue and apply the doily to the vase. Continue adding doilies in this way. Start with the largest ones and then use smaller ones to fill in the gaps. Cut some in half if necessary, to fill gaps at the top and bottom of the vase.

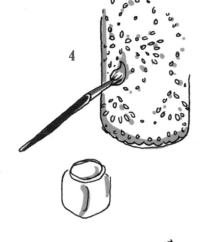

2 Paint the doilies with PVA working it into all the little holes. Let dry then paint the doily discs with decorator's varnish and let dry. Pick away any excess PVA and/ or varnish. Use a craft knife to lift off from the glass if necessary.

3 Add crystal drops, if using, to the rim of the vase by hanging from their metal drop hooks.

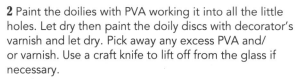

VARIATIONS

• For vases that are wider at the base than the top you can hang droplets from chains that sit around the narrower neck of the vase. Old bracelet chains or even delicate necklace chains doubled over, are perfect to hang crystals and other charms from, and can easily be removed when washing the vase.

Tile Tea Tray

Vintage ceramic tiles can be decorated with wonderful patterns and colors and whilst it might be tricky to find enough to cover a whole wall, if you discover just a handful then you can repurpose them into a uniquely stylish and practical serving tray.

YOU WILL NEED

Plywood ⅜in (12mm) thick, 19¾ x 13¾in (50 x 35cm)

6 vintage tiles, about 6-in (15-cm) square

Wood lengths, ¾ x ¾in (2 x 2cm): 2 x 18in (46cm) long and 2 x 13¾in (35cm) long

Hot glue gun

Drill, wood drill bit, countersink

2 x kitchen cabinet handles

Wood screws, about 1¼in (35mm) long

Tile spacers, ⅛in (3mm)

Grouting

Damp sponge

Wood paint and small paintbrush

1 Lay the plywood base down on a flat surface. Arrange your tiles in the center and place a tile spacer between each tile. Place one short length of wood on top of each short end of the base. Place one long length of wood on each long edge. Check that everything fits together. Don't worry if there is extra space around the tiles, as this can be filled in with grouting.

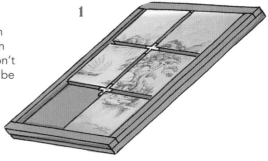

2 Remove the tiles and spacers. Using the hot glue gun, take one length of wood and apply glue to the underside and stick it back down into position and press firmly. Repeat with the other three lengths to create the edge of your tray.

3 Measure and mark the mid-point on top of one short length of wood. Place your handle over the top and make sure it is central. Mark the wood where the screw holes are in the handle. Repeat on the other short side. Drill a hole all the way through the wood and base at each of these four marks. Turn the tray over and countersink the holes on the base. This will allow your tray to lie flat once the screws are in position.

4 Position the tray on its side so that you can access the top and bottom simultaneously. Place a screw in one of the holes, entering from the base, and screw until the tip appears at the top edge. Align the handle hole, and screw home. Repeat with the other hole on this side to fix on the handle. Repeat with the other side.

5 Now you have made the tray, time to get tiling! With the tray flat, arrange your tiles using the spacers. Once in position, remove one tile and apply grouting to the reverse, reposition, and gently push down. Repeat with the other tiles. Let dry.

6 Remove the spacers. Now apply grouting to the gaps around the tiles. Use a damp sponge in a diagonal motion to remove any excess grouting. Let dry. If the grouting "shrinks" in drying, then reapply some more and let dry again.

7 Paint the wooden tray in your desired color. Use a smaller brush to get into tight corners and use a steady hand to paint up to the grouting in a straight line.

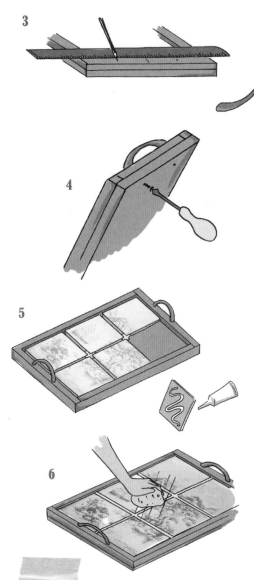

3

4

5

6

VARIATIONS

• Use vintage tin tiles for an industrial look.

• Use broken tiles and china to create a mosaic tray.

• If you don't want to make your own tray then re-use an old one and tile over the top of it. You could even pour in resin to create a flat tray surface.

Gardener's Kneeling Pad

Chapter 2 Vintage Kitchen and Garden

Discover ways to create vintage style indoors and out, including some great ideas for getting organized: the tea tray magnetic board (page 50) provides a great place to store notes, while the tea set bird feeders (page 58) will add accents of color in the garden.

Globe Fruit Bowl

Upcycled Silverware Hooks

I'm always finding beautiful silverware when rummaging at garage sales but the perennial problem is that they are never part of a complete set. These sad-looking odds and ends kick about in the bottom of often soggy, cardboard boxes but with this project we can save them from obscurity and turn them into something useful and unique!

YOU WILL NEED

Various silver forks (see step 1), preferably with a design or motif on the handle

OPTIONAL

Drill and drill bit

Pliers (with felt scraps or similar to cover plier teeth)

Hammer

1 Select your silverware. It is best if it's actually made of silver, as this is more malleable, so have a look on the back for the hallmark stamp—if it says EPNS or EP, this indicates it is electro-plated nickel silver and the core metal will be hard. It's still possible to bend this type of metal but you'll need a vice and a lot of elbow grease! You can use different designs but try to make sure the forks are roughly the same length so that your hooks end up the same size.

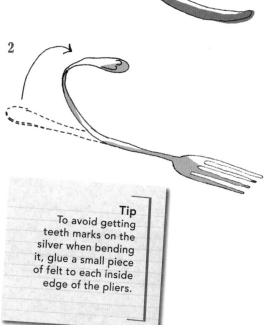

1

2

2 Either by hand or using pliers, bend the fork handle back about halfway to make a hanging hook. If the handle has a pattern, make sure the design becomes the front of the hook.

3 Flatten the fork head by placing the pliers over it and gently squeezing, working your way around so that you eventually flatten the whole area. If you have a vice then simply place the fork head inside, keeping the fork front and back parallel with the vice "walls," and then gently close the vice. If using silver, you could beat it flat with a hammer but be aware this could leave a pattern.

Tip
To avoid getting teeth marks on the silver when bending it, glue a small piece of felt to each inside edge of the pliers.

4 Drill a hole in the fork head so you can attach it to the wall. If you don't wish to drill a hole you could, using the pliers, bend the middle two fork prongs across each other to create a space in which to insert a screw.

5 Get creative and use the pliers to bend the remaining fork prongs into curls, loops, or whatever takes your fancy. For a simple bend, grip the fork prong firmly with the pliers (making sure that the end of the nose is roughly where you want your bend to be) and then pull down. For curls, start by gripping just the tip of the prong and bending with the pliers. Once you have made a small curl, move your pliers along the prong so that you are gripping either side of your curl (rather than the tip) and bend again.

6 Using a method suited to your wall (see page 122), fix the hook to the wall (or a length of wood to create a hook rack.

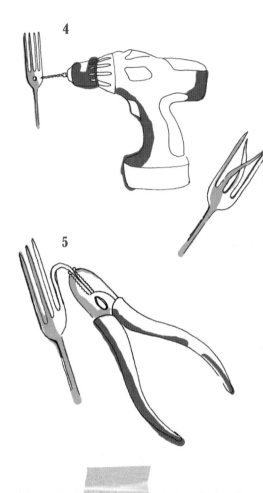

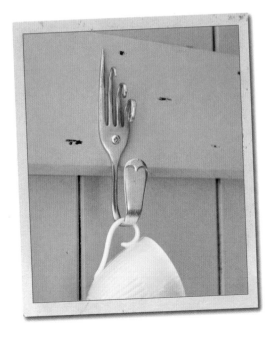

VARIATIONS

• Use a mixture of forks, spoons, and knives to create a more varied look.

• Use large serving utensils to make cabinet handles or coat hooks.

• Bend small dessert forks round to make napkin rings or even a bangle!

Dish Towel Curtains

Vintage dish towels come in such wonderful designs and colors that it often seems a shame to just relegate them to the humble task of drying the dishes. These are often items that people collected and then stored away, and occasionally you can find them in pristine condition with the inks as bright as the day they were printed. Sewn together they can make fantastic curtains for the window, under kitchen counters, or even as a tablecloth creating a fun "kitchenalia" look.

YOU WILL NEED

A collection of dish (tea) towels, preferably all the same size

Tape measure

Sewing machine and thread

Net curtain wire with hooks and eyes (or a thin curtain rod)

1 Measure the area for the curtain. First, measure the drop, from top to bottom. Now measure the width of the space you want to cover. Multiply the width by 2.5 if you want your curtains to hang in lovely gathers. For kitchen units, measure down from just under the countertop to the floor to ascertain your "drop" measurement.

> **Tip**
> Launder your dish towels before sewing as this will prevent any shrinkage and warping when washing your finished curtains in the future. Then press them flat with an iron.

2 Lay your dish towels on a large flat surface and measure out your drop and width measurements. Play around with the formation, try them portrait or landscape, or combinations of both until they nearly fit your measurements. They'll need to cover your drop plus at least about 3in (7cm) for a hem at the top. Bear in mind that you'll lose some length when they're sewn together, too. Widthwise there is loads of room for movement—less fabric means less folds, more fabric means more folds. You can also trim and re-hem if you wish. Consider the patterns and colors on the dish towels and aim for a balance.

3 For window curtains: pin two dish towels right sides together for each curtain and sew. I made a half window curtain and so joined two towels together along their long sides. For kitchen counters: pin all the dish towels together and sew along the seams to form one large piece of fabric. I used four dish towels and sewed two together, then the other two, and then finally pinned and sewed these larger pieces together to form the whole curtain. Press the seams open.

4 Lay the curtain face down. Measuring up from the bottom edge, fold over the top edge so that the measurement from the bottom to the top of the fold matches your drop. Press and pin the fold in place. As the dish towel is already hemmed, simply run a line of stitching just above the hem to form a channel at least 1¼in (3cm) wide for the curtain wire, or wider if you want to hang from a curtain rod.

5 Cut your curtain wire to the correct length and thread it through the channel at the top of your curtain. Attach the eyes onto each end of the wire (use eyes rather than hooks so they won't catch on your material when removing for washing). Screw in the hooks on either side of your unit or window and hang your curtain. You could also use a thin rod for hanging if you wish.

VARIATIONS:

• If you do not have suitable surfaces for screwing in hooks or mounting a curtain pole, you could use an expanding curtain rod instead.

• Make a tablecloth. If your dish towels are different sizes, find the smallest one and cut off the hem. Now cut your other dish towels down to match this size. Zigzag stitch (or overlock, if you can), along the edges to stop any fraying and then pin and sew together to make a rectangle that will cover your table. Press to flatten the seams. Cutting off the hems and edging them may be laborious but will result in a lovely flat tablecloth with no lumps and bumps—and best of all no-one else will have one quite like it!

Tea Tray Magnetic Board

This simple project shows you how to turn your favorite vintage tea tray into a useful bulletin board. Using a metal tray will allow you to attach magnets to hold notes or photos and create a beautiful focal point. I've used a plain silver-colored metal tray, but you could use a kitchenalia patterned tray for the kitchen or a bold design for the hallway—anywhere you want to leave notes, lists, or even just a collection of your best loved photos.

YOU WILL NEED

Vintage metal tray (not aluminum, the magnets won't stick!)

Ruler and pencil or marker pen

Wire wool or fine sandpaper (optional)

Drill and HSS drill bit

Ribbon (optional)

1 Once you've found a suitable tray, measure across the top to find the center point and make a small mark with a pencil or marker pen just below the top edge. This is where you will drill your hole for hanging.

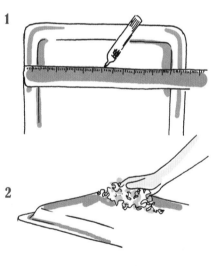

2 If your tray is polished metal you might want to knock some of the shine off it to dull it down. If so, rub lightly with fine sandpaper or wire wool to achieve the desired effect. Always test on the back of the tray first to avoid over scratching and to help you select the correct grade of wire wool or sandpaper.

3 Use a drill and drill bit to drill a hole through the tray at the point that you marked in step 1 (see page 120). Screw the tray to the wall using the hole you created or, alternatively, thread a ribbon through the hole and hang from a hook.

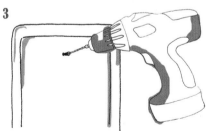

4 Now, dress your bulletin board with your favorite magnets, pictures, notes, and reminders.

VARIATION

• Match your magnets with your ribbon for a coordinated look.

Gardener's Kneeling Pad

Most keen gardeners spend a certain amount of time on their knees in the dirt, tackling weeds and tending the borders. By transforming a scrap of pre-loved fabric into a waterproof material to make into a practical kneeling pad, you can banish damp knees forever! It even comes complete with a handle that you can use to move it around, pick it up, or hang it in the shed.

YOU WILL NEED

Pre-loved fabric, about ½yd (½m)

Self-adhesive transparent vinyl (such as Fablon)

Sewing machine and matching thread

Old cloth, such as a dish (tea) towel, for ironing

Iron

Padding—foam or unwanted plastic bags

1 Cut a piece of fabric 19 x 19in (48 x 48cm) and place it right side up on a hard, flat surface. Cut a piece of the vinyl slightly larger than your fabric. Peel the backing paper away from one edge for about 4in (10cm) and stick this along one edge of the fabric, making sure it is straight—you can peel it off and re-apply if not. Start to pull more of the backing paper away, smoothing down the vinyl as you go until you have covered all of your fabric. Trim off any excess vinyl around the edges.

1

2 With the fabric facing you and with the design the right way up, fold the fabric in half by lifting the bottom corners up to meet the top ones. Pin at right angles along the two short sides.

2

3 Starting from the folded edge, sew along each side taking a ½in (1cm) seam. Stop sewing ½in (1cm) from the top edge. Fold back the top, unstitched edge by ½in (1cm) and press using an old cloth to protect the vinyl. Turn right way out.

3

4 To make the handle strap, cut a piece of fabric 16 x 10in (40 x 4cm) and cover it with vinyl as you did in step 2. With the right side facing down, fold the long bottom edge in by a third, then fold the top edge over the top and pin in place. Stitch centrally along the length of your fabric strip.

5 Fold the handle in half and insert the ends about ¾in (2cm) inside the top seam of the cover in the right-hand corner. To avoid having to stitch through too many layers, position the strap ends side by side and pin in place. Sew along the top seam just over the handles. If it's very thick you may need to turn the sewing machine handle by hand.

6 Stuff the cover with scrunched up plastic bags until it feels nicely padded, or use a piece of foam cut slightly smaller than your cover. Machine stitch along the top seam of the cover to finish, stopping just before the handle.

VARIATIONS

• Re-use fabric from an old PVC apron or tablecloth, which are already waterproofed.

• Use synthetic rope, nylon webbing, or other waterproof trim for the handle.

• Use a contrasting color thread for your stitches.

• Use what you have for the filling: old pillows or pillow pads, even bundles of rags would all do the job!

• Fit a zipper along the top edge and create a waterproof travel bag!

Teapot Hanging Planters

It's always a sad moment when a beloved teapot becomes redundant after getting a chip or a crack, but with this simple idea you can turn it into a clever planter and give it a completely new lease of life. Build up a collection of fancy chipped china and group them together on the patio, stagger them up the garden steps, or simply hang them up for a whimsical display.

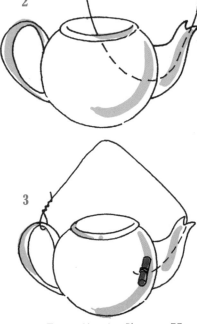

YOU WILL NEED

Teapot without lid

Garden wire

Wire cutters

Dowling (or similar)

Long nails (5in/12cm long or more)

Hammer

Potting compost and plants

Gravel for drainage (optional)

1 Cut a length of garden wire about 40in (1m) long and thread one end down through the teapot spout so that it emerges inside the teapot.

2 Reach inside the teapot, take hold of the wire, and gently pull it part way through so that there is some slack to work with. Take a piece of dowling about 2in (5cm) long and wrap the wire around the center and tie it off. You could use wooden lollipop sticks or even cotton bobbins or large buttons—anything that will sit across the inside of the spout and stop the wire from coming out.

3 Pull the wire back gently so that the dowling meets the inside of the spout, then take the other end of the wire and thread it through the handle. Wrap the wire around itself and trim off any excess with the wire cutters.

4 Now simply place your plant pot in the teapot, adding some gravel in the base for drainage, if needed, or planting in potting compost.

5 Hammer a long nail into the wall as a hanging hook—the nail should protrude out from the wall so that the teapot will hang straight down and not lean in toward the wall. Position the wire close to the nail head. To adjust the height that the teapot hangs, skip step 3 and adjust the length of the hanging wire before fastening it off on the teapot handle once in position.

VARIATION

• For a plant pot, simply add your plant or herbs and position on a windowsill or the patio for all to enjoy.

Tea Set Bird Feeders

A wonderful way to use sweet vintage tea cups and saucers that have been chipped is to turn them into these gorgeous china bird feeders. Place or hang them around the garden for your feathery friends to feast on—they'll look great with the teapot planters on page 55, too!

page 55

YOU WILL NEED

Old cups and saucers, matching or not

Pencil

Cloth-backed coarse grade sandpaper

All-purpose glue or hot glue gun

Fishing line, or hanging hooks for bird feeders, available from specialty stores

Tip
If you feel confident using a glue gun you can use it to glue the two pieces together but be aware that the hot glue sets in a matter of seconds, so you'll have to bring the pieces together accurately and swiftly.

1 With your saucer flat on a work surface, position the cup on its side on the saucer with the handle facing skyward. Position the cup so that the handle is as upright as can be and mark with a pencil on both the cup and saucer where their surfaces meet.

2 Using the coarse sandpaper, gently sand the marked areas on the cup and saucer to remove the glaze and expose the ceramic beneath—this will create a better surface for your glue to adhere to. Don't worry if you sand away your pencil marks, it doesn't have to be exact. Brush away any sanding dust.

3 Apply a thin layer of glue onto each area that you've sanded and wait 10–15 minutes for it to become tacky.

4

4 Position your cup on the saucer, checking from all angles that the cup is centrally placed—the handle is pointing upward and not tilting to one side and the cup is in the center of the saucer and not off to one side so that it will hang well once finished. Push together firmly. The glue will harden in 2–4 hours.

5 To hang the feeder, thread some thick fishing line through the handle and tie off, leaving a length to tie from a tree branch.

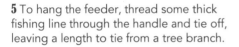

VARIATIONS

• An alternative way to hang the feeders is from a feeder pole. This is a spike you drive into the ground that has a hook at the top, rather like a shepherd's crook. Simply hang the cup handle over the hook.

• You can extend this technique to create all sorts of configurations. Another cup glued rim down to a saucer or plate could be attached below to create a separate compartment for water or seeds.

Cheese Grater Pen Pot

Rusty or blunt cheese graters may no longer be useful for preparing food but reworked and re-imagined they can become useful pots and holders for all manner of items whilst still retaining that vintage rustic charm. Get organized and use one as a pencil pot and add a little dish below for a pencil sharpener or paper clips.

YOU WILL NEED

Vintage metal cheese grater with flat handle	Nut and bolt (¼in/5mm thread, length ½in/1cm)
Mini jello mold or metal flan dish	Wood or hardboard (at least ⅛in/3mm thick)
Marker pen	Spray enamel paint
Drill and metal drill bits (sizes 2.5, 4, and 5)	

1 With the cheese grater the right way up, measure and mark the mid-point of the handle. Using the smallest metal drill bit, drill a hole through the mark (see page 120). Turn the jello mold upside down, and measure and mark the center point on the base. Drill a hole through the mark.

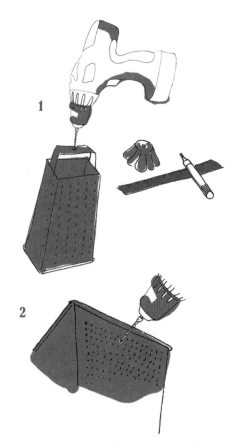

2 With the wide side of the grater facing you (the one with the smaller holes), mark the center point across, about 2 rows of holes down from the top. Drill a hole using the small drill bit. Alternatively, you could use the side with the larger holes to hang from, even using an existing hole to hook onto a hanging hook or nail.

3 Change your drill bit for a larger size and re-drill the holes in the handle, jello mold, and reverse of the grater. Change again for a larger size drill bit and repeat.

4 Place the grater upside down (handle downward) with the back facing you. Lay the pens that you want to display next to the grater and decide how much (if any) of the pens you want to see poking over the top once the grater is mounted on the wall. Note the measurement from the top of the grater to the base of the pen.

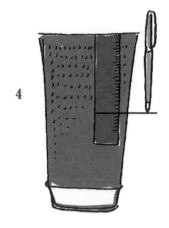

5 At the point noted in step 4, measure the width across and at the side and cut a piece of wood to this measurement to make your internal "shelf." Carefully drop the wooden block in from the widest point of the grater and push it down until it will not go any further.

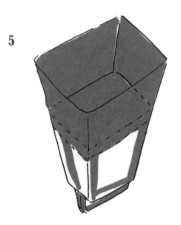

6 Thread the bolt through the hole in the mold with the bolt head inside. Position the dish so that it nestles inside the upside down grater handle and push the thread down through the hole in the handle. Attach the nut and tighten.

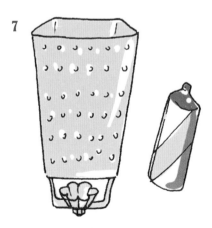

7 Working in a well-ventilated area, spray paint your pen pot, ensuring an even coat with short bursts of paint and remembering the inside of the handle and mold. Hang from the wall using the hole on the back that you pre-drilled earlier.

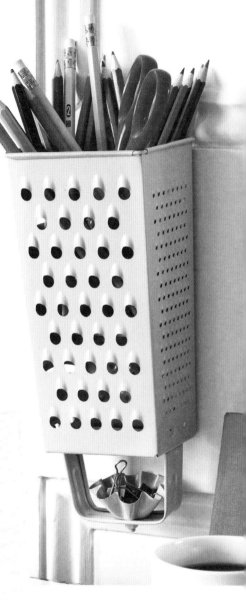

VARIATIONS

• Drill small holes through the handle and bolt on small cup hooks so that you can hang other useful items from the base.

• Hang next to your bulletin board to keep pens at hand. If you use a steel grater it can also store spare magnets for your board, too.

• Leave it unpainted for a rustic and quirky look in the kitchen and use it to store your cooking utensils. Make and hang several together for some striking storage solutions.

• Pop a ball of string inside and feed the loose end out through one of your holes to make a handy string dispenser. Pull out your desired length of string and cut off what you need, leaving a little excess for next time.

Globe Fruit Bowl

Vintage globes are having a resurgence in popularity at the moment and whilst country borders and names evolve, they may not be up to date as an educational aid but can still be used as a fantastic decorative object. Turn a hemisphere into a large fruit bowl or even a hanging light pendant for a touch of globetrotting glamour.

YOU WILL NEED

Vintage globe (preferably tin or cardboard but you can use plastic too)

Hacksaw

Sandpaper

Masking tape

Old newspapers

Spray enamel paint

Vintage clear glass ashtray or similar

Hot glue gun

1 Remove the globe from any mounting. Cut the globe in half using a hacksaw, holding it carefully. For tin globes, use a metal saw blade. Use the equator as your guideline and if your globe has a "lip" around the middle, cut above this so you keep it as the edge of your bowl. Sand the cut edge to get rid of any sharp edges.

2 Clean the globe to remove any dust, dirt, or grease. Prepare your work area for spray painting. Mask off the globe exterior with masking tape and old newspapers. Working in a well-ventilated space, spray the interior with your spray paint. Let dry. As the paint dries it may slide down the globe, so keep applying thin layers and allowing them to dry until the interior is covered.

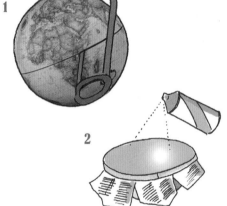

3 Mask the top edge of the glass ashtray and spray the inside with the spray paint and let dry. Repeat if necessary.

4 Turn the ashtray upside down. Place the globe on top, taking note of where the two meet and apply hot glue to this point. Reposition the globe and press firmly down to assemble the bowl.

VARIATIONS
- Make a pendant light shade using the other hemisphere.
- Decoupage the inside of the globe bowl with paper maps to continue the look.

Crate Bedside Table

Chapter 3 **Vintage Bedroom and Bathroom**

Here you'll find both luxury statement pieces, such as the beautiful brocade bolsters (page 77) that are made from vintage embellished fabric, and subtler, practical projects, like the pillowcase laundry bag (page 84).

Pillowcase Laundry Bag

Mirror Makeover

Vintage mirrors are usually made with thick glass and mounted on even thicker wood. Sturdy and strong, certainly, but they can also look a bit dowdy and, well, out of date! This method allows you to add modern designs and patterns to revamp your mirror into a brilliant fusion of old and new, creating a beautiful focal point whilst retaining its original usefulness. Gorgeous!

YOU WILL NEED

Vintage mirror

Screwdriver

Patterned fabric or paper

Scissors

Spray mount

Paper or card

Tracing paper

Pencil

Chinograph or marker pen

Safety goggles

Flat, square, sharp craft blades and holder or scraper

All-purpose glue

1 Remove the mirror from the wooden back by unscrewing the fixings (or remove it from the frame). Clean the back of the mirror so that it is free from dirt and dust.

1

2 Gently iron your fabric, if using. Lay your fabric (or paper) over the front of the mirror and decide which elements of the pattern you want to feature.

3

3 Cut around your chosen elements, leaving a large border of about 2in (5cm) or more, and roughly following the outline of the shape. Working in a well-ventilated space, spray mount the fabric shape onto white paper or thin card (making sure you glue the reverse of the fabric and not your design side) and let dry.

4 Lay a sheet of tracing paper on your mounted fabric and trace around the parts of the design you want to see through the glass. Then cut this shape out from the tracing paper (stick it to paper or card first if it makes it easier to handle).

5 Now flip the tracing over and place it in position on the back of your mirror (it should look like the reverse image of your proposed design). Once in position, lightly spray mount and tack it in place. Draw around the tracing with a chinagraph pencil.

6 Remove the tracing paper and begin to scrape away the mirror backing inside your outline, using a flat, square blade in a craft knife. Older mirrors are backed with three layers; the silvering layer directly on the glass, a copper layer, and finally the backing paint layer. As you scrape you will first take off the paint layer but not the silvering perhaps. Protect your eyes from any chips of paint with safety goggles.

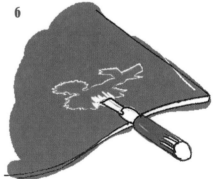

7 Then, very carefully, use a sharp blade flat to the surface to remove the copper and silvering layers. If you want to remove large areas of silvering then consider using a "Mirror Silvering Remover" product. The silver layer will take some effort to scrape away but persevere—it will be worth it! It doesn't have to be perfect. Periodically turn the mirror over and place your design behind to check how you are progressing.

7

8 Now apply some glue to the back of the mirror, roughly 1in (2.5cm) outside the edge of the scraped area, and gently apply your paper-backed design. Turn the mirror over and adjust the alignment of your paper design until it is in place. Turn the mirror back and allow the glue to dry.

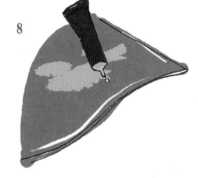

8

9 Once dry, trim any paper that protrudes over the edge of the mirror with scissors. Place the mirror back into it's frame and reassemble. Voila!

VARIATIONS

• Patterned wallpapers, gift wrap, and other paper ephemera are good alternatives, or print out images using your home printer.

• If using fabric, wrap strips tightly around the hanging chain to continue the look.

• To adapt the idea for a kid's room, leave reflective mirror in the center so they can see their faces and add an astronaut's helmet or princess headdress image to the rest of the mirror. When they look in it they will see themselves transformed!

Vintage Lace *Shower Curtain*

It's easy to add vintage elegance to a bathroom with a few well-chosen accessories but I find that shower curtains, sleek and modern by design, can dominate the room and dictate the overall "look." For a vintage statement, try combining the functionality and practicality of a modern curtain with the elegance and handmade look of a lace tablecloth.

YOU WILL NEED

Shower curtain

Vintage lace tablecloths or tray cloths and doilies

Shower curtain rings with clips

Shower pole

1 Using a brightly colored shower curtain as your base, lay this out flat and position your lace tablecloth over the top. It's fine if it doesn't cover the shower curtain all the way from top to bottom but it should cover it from side to side. If you need to, sew two or more tablecloths together until the panel is big enough. You could even sew lots of smaller lace items together, like doilies or tray cloths, until you have a large enough panel.

2 Lay out your shower curtain rings with clips along the width of the top of your curtain, adjusting them until they are evenly spaced. If you can't find shower rings with pincer clips then make your own by using metal shower curtain rings and thread a small metal bulldog clip onto each ring.

3 Starting at one end, use the clips to pinch the shower curtain and lace panel together. If you prefer, you can clip the shower curtain first and then go back along feeding the lace into each clip to attach the lace panel.

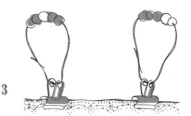

4 Thread the rings onto your shower curtain pole and hang your elegant curtain for an instant bathroom makeover. If you'd like to shorten the curtain and/or lace you can simply unclip, fold over along the top, and then re-clip to adjust.

VARIATIONS

• If a brightly colored shower curtain doesn't appeal, use a pale shade instead for a more subtle look.

• You could use anything to make the panel—try doilies or crocheted textiles to allow your shower curtain color to peep through, or even use vintage silk scarves sewn together and a plain, pale shower curtain hidden behind.

Soap Dispenser Jars

Vintage preserve jars inherently have tons of character and it's a shame to keep them just in the kitchen or pantry! Here is a project to turn them (and other vessels) into quirky yet stylish liquid soap dispensers that look great in the best bathroom, cloakroom, or even potting shed.

YOU WILL NEED

Glass jars with metal or plastic lids

Soap dispenser pump (available from craft stores, online, or reuse one from an old dispenser)

Ruler and marker pen or pencil

Drill and HSS drill bit or

hammer and large nail

Liquid soap

OPTIONAL

Enamel paint and paintbrush

Clear lacquer or varnish

Hot glue gun

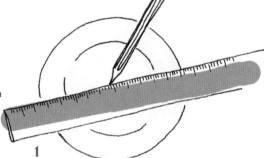

1 Select your jar and make sure it is clean and has a metal or plastic lid (rather than a ceramic or glass one that you can't make a hole in easily). Measure across the lid to find the center and mark this point.

2 To make the hole in the lid, remove the lid, clamp it down, and drill through your center mark. Use a drill bit that will make a big enough hole for your soap dispenser pump tube to fit into. If you don't want to drill and are using a metal lid you can make a hole using a hammer and nail. Keep working the edges until you have a large enough hole (this method will be easier if you have the lid screwed onto the jar). Check the dispenser tube fits in the hole and the top of the dispenser sits comfortably on the lid—if the plastic tube is too long, simply trim it a little until it fits.

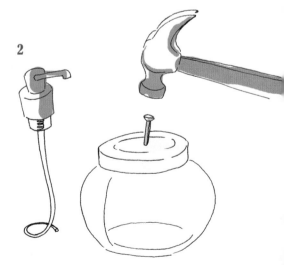

3 You can paint your lid to match your dispenser for a more professional look. I used a Mason (Kilner) jar that had a gold lid but my dispenser was brushed steel, so I painted the lid in a silver enamel paint so it would blend in. Separate the lid parts (if it has them) and give each part 2–3 coats of enamel and then seal with a clear lacquer, leaving enough time to dry between each coat.

4 If you have measured the dispenser correctly and made the right-sized hole, you can push the dispenser into the hole and it will stay there. If not, don't worry as you can glue them together to seal them in place. Carefully apply the hot glue around the inside edge of the dispenser and push onto the lid. Hold in place for a few minutes. Once the glue has cooled and set, you can simply pick off any excess.

5 Fill the jar with your favorite liquid soap and screw on the lid. Your soap dispenser is ready to grace the most stylish of bathrooms.

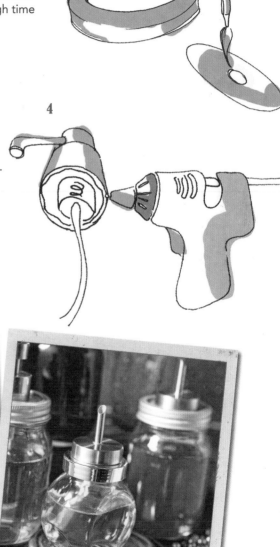

Brocade Bolster

Find inspiration in decorated panels from vintage evening and cocktail dresses, use embroidery from the back of dressing gowns, brocade from bridesmaid dresses, or any other fancy fabric that you can find to create these luxury bedroom bolsters.

YOU WILL NEED

Vintage embellished fabric, such as an embroidered dressing gown back, wedding dress, or evening dress

Complementary fabric for backing

Cotton lining fabric (optional)

Sewing machine

Overlocker (optional)

Rectangular bolster form, I used 12 x 36in (30 x 91.5cm) —use feathers for comfort

1 Gently hand wash your fabrics and press them so they are nice and flat. If your fabric is delicate, use the cotton lining or other clean fabric over the top when pressing. Measure your bolster pad from seam to seam along the length and width.

2 Measure and cut your fabric for the front, to the bolster dimensions plus 1in (2.5cm) seam allowance on all sides. If your fabric is delicate or a brocade that has lots of threads on the reverse, cut out a piece of cotton lining to the same size. Cut out the backing fabric to the same dimensions.

3 Lay your backing fabric right side up and place the front fabric on top with right side down. Position the lining fabric on top, if using. Pin all three layers together along the top, left side and bottom edge, 1in (2.5cm) from the edge.

4 Machine stitch the three sides together. For neatness, overlock these three sides or, if you do not have access to an overlocker, trim ½in (1cm) of excess fabric and zigzag stitch the three layers together along the raw edges.

5 Turn the cover right side out through the open side and push out the corners gently, using the blunt end of a knitting needle if necessary. Insert the bolster form, aligning the bolster corners with the cover corners and work the bolster in until it fits.

6 Fold under the raw edges at the opening by 1in (2.5cm) and pin. Slip stitch the cover closed using a matching thread.

5

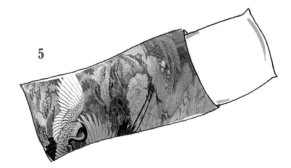

6

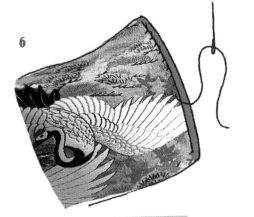

VARIATIONS

• If you don't have enough material to make a long bolster then adapt your measurements to fit a smaller rectangular or square pillow form.

• Use unembellished fabric parts rescued from the same garment for your backing fabric.

• Choose embellished fabrics that complement each other for both sides of your bolster, to create a double-sided pillow that you can just flip over when you fancy a change!

• Use vintage embroidered or cutwork table runners for your cover and use a colored lining fabric to peep through the holes.

Crochet Headboard

Few things are more opulent than a beautifully upholstered headboard. They can turn a plain bedroom into a relaxing and welcoming haven, add a touch of luxury, or make a bold statement. This project shows you how to make a padded headboard from scratch and then cover it with a vintage crochet blanket. If you get bored of it or change your décor you can simply change your headboard cover to match!

1 Place your cut MDF board on a flat surface. Position the foam on top of the board and trim it very neatly, if necessary, so that you have about 1in (2.5cm) extending over the edge on all sides. If you don't have one large piece of foam, use smaller pieces with straight edges and butt them up against each other until you have covered the board, again leaving 1in (2.5cm) excess.

2 Apply glue to the board and reposition the foam on top and let it set.

3 Iron your lining fabric—I chose a piece of light-colored linen as it's strong and the paleness creates a clean backdrop for where it shows through the crochet. You can use any color and pattern that you like and any fabric that will take a bit of tension. Lay the fabric out flat right side down on a large work surface or the floor and position the board on top, centrally with the foam facing down.

YOU WILL NEED

Sheet of MDF or chipboard, cut to size (see Tip)

Foam—enough to cover board plus 1in (2.5cm) extra on all sides, the thicker the foam, the deeper the headboard

All-purpose glue

Lining fabric, same size as your board plus at least 4in (10cm) extra on all sides—a solid linen or cotton fabric will work well

Staple gun (and staple remover)

Vintage crochet blanket

Mirror plates and screws, to fix

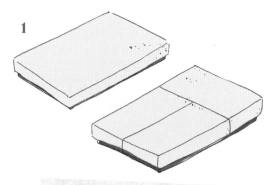

> **Tip**
> To calculate the size of your headboard, measure the width of your bed and allow approximately 25½in (65cm) for the headboard height, plus the depth of your mattress. My headboard was 33½in (85cm) high in total.

4 Starting in the center of the top edge, gently pull the fabric over the foam and staple through it onto the back of the board. Repeat in the center of the bottom edge, and the center of the two sides. This helps set the fabric tension across the headboard. The excess foam at the edges changes shape under the pressure of the stretched fabric and forms a nice curve.

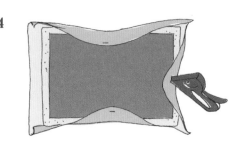

5 Continue adding staples, working out from the center on each side, until you have just the corners left. Leave some space here for creating your corner folds, you can always staple any gaps at the end.

6 Corners! Don't panic, there's an easy way to do this. Bring your fabric from each side together so it meets in a line that's 45 degrees from the corner. Pull to keep the tension and staple along each side.

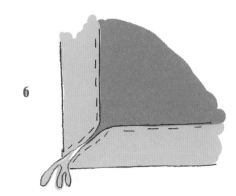

7 Now trim the excess fabric away along the stapled lines—you can cut quite close to the staples. Stop trimming just before you get to the corner. Pull out the excess fabric you have left that's still attached and trim it down into a triangular flap.

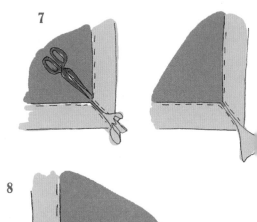

8 Now, pulling the fabric taut, fold the flap back over your 45-degree staple lines and staple it in place. This should produce a neat corner that will lie flat against the wall when the headboard is mounted.

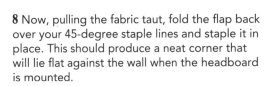

9 Repeat steps 4–8 using your crochet blanket. To make sure that the pattern isn't wonky, start with the board propped up and place your blanket over the headboard, moving it around until you find the best position. Put some holding staples in along the back of the top edge. Now rotate the board so that bottom edge is at the top. Pull gently on the blanket, align the pattern, and put in holding staples. Repeat with the two shorter sides. Check the front—if the pattern is straight, continue adding staples to secure. If not, try gently pulling the blanket into position and see if a few strategic staples will help or if you need to remove the staples and start again.

9

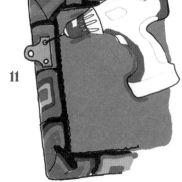

10 Repeat steps 6–8 to complete the corners. If you don't want to cut your blanket, just fold the excess material as flat as you can and staple down. Be aware that the headboard might not sit as flush against the wall.

11 To attach the headboard, measure down one third of the board height from the top on both short sides and screw in some mirror plates. It's fine to screw through the fabric, just make sure the screws bite well into the wood to create a good hold. See page 122 on how to mount the headboard to the wall behind your bed.

11

VARIATIONS

• You can use almost any fabric to create your headboard. Use a lining fabric to take the strain against the foam then you can use delicate fabrics over the top without tearing them. Lace, silks, or brocades would all look stunning.

• Ikat rugs can make striking headboards—just make sure you upgrade your scissors and staple gun to "heavy duty" so that they can handle the thicker woven fabric.

• Fancy a change? Simply use a staple remover to remove the staples from the top cover and replace it with a new fabric.

Pillowcase *Laundry Bag*

Searching through linens at a flea market or yard sale can often reveal solitary pillowcases with pretty prints or embroidery on them, which can be transformed into this practical drawstring laundry bag. Vintage pillowcases have usually been washed many times, which makes them very soft—perfect for transporting delicate items like lingerie when traveling.

Tip
Use the bag as an eco-friendly Furoshiki (Japanese gift wrapping cloth) to wrap bottles or other gifts for friends and invite them to pass it on!

YOU WILL NEED

A pretty vintage pillowcase

Stitch ripper

Sewing machine

Sewing needle and matching thread

2yd (2m) rope cord

Safety pin

1 The pillowcase is made up of two sides. Side A has the longer fabric folded over that you tuck the pillow inside. Side B just has a hem, probably about ¾in (2cm) deep. At one of the top corners where these two sides meet, take the stitch ripper and rip open the stitching that joins side A to side B, just along the seam line down to the hem on side B. Remove any remaining threads.

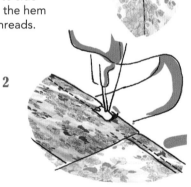

2 Machine stitch a line across side A to match the original hemline of side B. You have now formed the channel for the drawstring. Secure the machine threads at the beginning and end of your stitching.

3 Return to where you ripped open the stitching. Fold the raw edge of side B back inside the open hem and backstitch it in place. The edge of side A will be folded back on itself already but run a line of backstitch around it to match that of side B and to secure the edge. Once you reach the point where the two sides meet, put in a few extra stitches to strengthen this join.

4 Fasten a safety pin through one end of the cord. Feed the safety pin through the channel, gathering up the fabric as you feed it through. If you meet resistance at the seam halfway along, then try wiggling it through. If the sides are sewn together, use the stitch ripper to undo a few stitches to allow the cord to travel through. Add a couple of stitches here to strengthen the join at the edges of the channel. Keep going until the end of the cord re-emerges.

4

5 Pull some of the cord through and then remove the pin. Pull the cord through the channel until you have an even amount of cord coming out of both holes.

6

6 Knot the two ends of the cord together and pull tight to secure the knot. Pull the cord through the fabric to gather the top of the bag. Trim any frayed cord ends with scissors: to prevent further fraying you can dip the ends in clear nail varnish. You now have a beautiful drawstring bag for your smalls!

VARIATIONS

• Use pretty ribbon instead of cord for the drawstring.

• Make a smaller bag by turning the pillowcase inside out and sewing straight across at your desired height. Trim off the excess and turn the right way out again.

• If cutting down, use the excess fabric to make smaller bags for gifts or pot pourri pouches.

• Personalize by adding initials to the side or decorate with ribbons, buttons, or badges.

Ladder Back Chair Towel Rail

A great way to re-purpose a broken or odd ladder back chair is to turn it into a towel rail and tidy for the bathroom or cloakroom. It's the perfect size to fit into a small space for hanging hand towels and the cute shelf will maximize storage for your essential potions and lotions. Customize with a lick of paint and some decorative knobs to complete the transformation.

YOU WILL NEED

Wooden ladder back chair (with drop-in seat)

Yard stick (meter ruler)

Pencil

Hand saw

Wooden batten, ¾ x ¾in (2 x 2cm) x width of seat

Drill, wood drill bits, countersink

Wood screws

Bull-nosed pliers

Sandpaper (optional)

Wood paint and paintbrush

2 decorative knobs

Hot glue gun

1 Remove the seat from the chair. Turn the chair upside down, placing the seat frame on your work surface with the back of the chair hanging down over the edge. Measure back from each chair leg to the depth of your shelf, place the long ruler across the chair at these points, and draw a cutting line on the seat frame. Repeat for the support rail too, if your chair has one, as this will make a useful shelf rail. Alternatively, use a straight piece of wood the same depth as your shelf and butt it up against the chair legs. Draw along the other side to make your cutting mark.

2 Using the hand saw, cut along your pencil lines. Remove the piece you have cut away (the front of the chair and front two legs). Now measure and mark along the back legs where you want to cut them down. You can cut them flush with the seat frame, the support rails, or leave a little extending above. Cut along the marked lines.

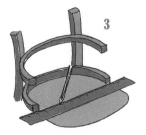

3 Take your seat and, if it is covered, remove the holding staples with bull-nosed pliers and remove the cover to reveal the wooden base. Place the seat back into position and, using your ruler, draw a line across the seat in line with the cut frame edge.

4 Cut a batten from the ¾ x ¾in (2 x 2cm) wood to the width of your seat. Line up the cut edge of your seat with the edge of the batten and drill pilot holes for your fixing screws. As this forms the shelf surface, you want it as flat as possible so countersink the holes in your seat so that the screw heads can lie flat.

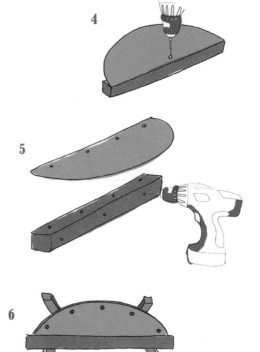

5 Now drill guidance holes into the batten on the parallel axis to the seat. These are for fixing to the wall later on but do them now while you have room for the drill head to get into the tight spot. Use wood screws to screw the seat to the batten.

6 On the underside of the seat, drill 5 or 6 pilot holes evenly spaced along the curved side, just in from the edge. You can countersink them too, if you wish, although they will be underneath the shelf and out of sight. Position the seat shelf back into the seat frame (with the batten underneath) and, guided by your pilot holes, screw your seat to the chair frame.

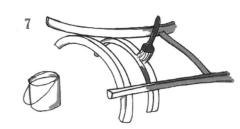

7 Sand any rough edges to smooth out your wood and to create a good key for painting. Paint with a wood paint, making sure to avoid any drips. I used two coats. You can also distress the paint by sanding back into it on the edges to achieve a worn vintage look (see the Louvred Art Gallery, page 99).

8 Mount a decorative knob onto each cut chair leg end. Ceramic or glass knobs can be pretty. Fix in place using a hot glue gun and let set.

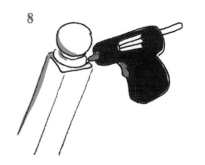

9 Your ladder back chair towel rail is now ready to be fixed to the wall. Use the pre-drilled holes in the batten to fix it in place (see page 122).

Crate Bedside Table

Vintage apple crates are a favorite of mine. Made in a pre-plastic era, they were sturdily constructed, have a wonderful patina, and sometimes the faint remnants of the original manufacturer's stamp hinting at their long history and heritage. Oozing industrial and rustic charm, they can be used in so many rooms of the home. This project shows you how to customize and decorate your own crate to transform it into a unique bedside unit.

YOU WILL NEED

Vintage wooden crate or box

Sandpaper

MDF or plywood, approx ⅝in (1.5cm) thick, cut to fit inside (ask the lumber yard to cut to your required size)

2 pieces of wood for supports, ¾ x ¾in (2 x 2cm) x depth of crate

Drill and wood drill bit

Screws

Spirit level

Decorative paper

Spray mount

Hammer and panel pins

Toughened glass, at least ¼in (5mm) thick, cut to size A (see step 2), with edges beveled

Glass clamps or brackets (optional), see step 10

1 Clean and check over your crate, removing any rogue nails and sanding any rough edges. Stand the crate on one of the short ends with the opening toward you. Test both ends to see which is the flattest and place this end at the top so that the glass will sit flat.

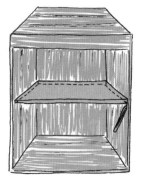

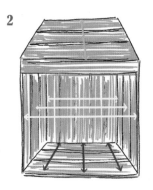

2 Measure the width and depth of the top and decide where you'd like your glass to be, either flush with the edge or slightly smaller. Note this measurement (A). Now measure the crate internally, width first. To add one shelf halfway up, measure across the crate at this point and mark in pencil. Take a few measurements in case the crate is wonky and note the smallest measurement (B). Measure the depth, again taking a few measurements. I recommend that the shelf stops ½in (1cm) in from the front edge of the crate but you may prefer it to be flush with the edges. Note this measurement (C).

3 Ask a lumber yard to cut your MDF to the measurements B x C for the shelf. Now measure the thickness of the shelf and mark this onto the inside of the crate. You can either measure down from your center mark to do this or hold your shelf in position (with the top edge of the shelf in line with your centre mark inside the crate) and draw along the bottom of the shelf. Put the shelf to one side.

4 Cut the support wood down to measurement C, minus ¾in (2cm). Cutting it slightly shorter will help hide the supports from view. Hold each piece inside the crate, just below your center mark and with the back of the support touching the back of the crate. Mark the center of each crate slat on the supports. Drill pilot holes centrally at each of these three points on both supports. Make the hole large enough that the screw can slot into it without being screwed.

5 Place a screw in each of the 3 holes of one support. Line up the top of the support with your newer, lower center mark, and fix the screws in so that they bite into the slats of the crate. Rest your shelf on this support and hold up your other batten in position with the shelf resting on it for a quick spot check to see if things are on track. Fix the other support in place, using a spirit level and adjusting the position if necessary until the shelf lies flat.

6 To cover the shelf, line up the top edge of your paper with the back edge of the shelf. Allow at least 2in (5cm) extra at both sides and at least 4in (10cm) at the front edge. Trim the paper to size. Make sure your shelf is dust and dirt free. Working in a well-ventilated space, spray mount the back of the paper, realign it on the shelf with the edges overlapping, and smooth down.

VARIATIONS

• Use wallpaper leftovers or samples instead of gift wrap, or make your own memento collages from photos and paper ephemera.

• Wall mount the unit by fixing brackets underneath to achieve the perfect bedside height (see page 122).

• Paint inside the crate with complementary colors to enhance the designs on your paper.

• Group several smaller boxes together to create an interesting storage feature.

7 Smooth and glue the paper over the front edge of your shelf right round onto the underside. Fold the paper along the lines extending from the corners of your shelf and trim away the square of paper from the underside edge to the bottom fold. Now cut along the other fold to make a thin flap that you stick along the edge of the shelf. Cut the corner off at a diagonal. Spray mount and stick down around the side of the shelf and onto the underside. Gently pull as you stick so it's nice and flush. You can cover the underside too, if you wish.

8 Position your shelf inside the crate on top of the supports. Fix it in place with panel pins by hammering them down from the top surface into the battens below.

9 Lay out another sheet of decorative paper right side up on a flat, clean work surface and place the glass for the top of your crate over it. Move the glass around until it covers a pattern you'd like to display and mark around the edge of the glass with a pencil. Cut out the paper with scissors. Position the paper on the top of the crate and add the glass top. You could add another piece of glass on top of your shelf, too, if you wish.

10 For extra safety, you can secure the glass top to the crate with glass clamps or brackets, which are available from hardware stores. If doing so, take account of how these clamps attach to the wood and make allowances for them in your measurements when deciding on the size of your glass top.

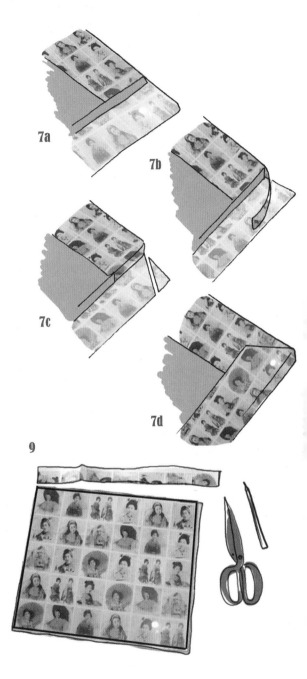

7a

7b

7c

7d

9

Découpage Suitcase

Chapter 4 Vintage Children's Rooms

These clever upcycling ideas show you how to create gorgeous yet practical storage solutions, as well as toys that children will love. Display treasured drawings with a louvred art gallery (page 99), or make a hula hoop hideout (page 117) that will bring hours of fun, as well as being easy to pack away once playtime is over!

Toy Bookends

Play Stove

The beauty of upcycling is seeing potential in an item. When I found this old bedside cabinet it just screamed "play stove" at me because of its shape—the little door, even a small drawer that was perfect for fixing the "hob controls" onto—and so I brought it home. I told my son it was a play stove and that's all he really needed to start "cooking" on it, but I knew it could really look the part with a fairly simple makeover. Here's how to create the transformation.

YOU WILL NEED

A bedside cabinet or small unit with door

Sandpaper

Primer

4 x round cork placemats or coasters

Black paint

Varnish or lacquer

Knobs and fixings

Water-based paint and paintbrushes

Ruler

Glue or hot glue gun

Optional

TSP (sugar soap)

Enamel paint for knobs

Drill and wood drill bit

Screwdriver

1 Lightly sand the unit and make sure the surface is free from dirt, dust, and grease. TSP (sugar soap) is good for this but check the label for instructions. Apply a coat of primer to the unit and let dry.

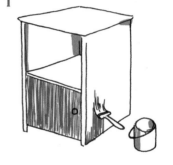

2 While the cabinet is drying, take your cork coasters and paint the edges and one surface of each with black paint. You could either use black enamel paint or acrylic paint, sealed with a coat of varnish when dry. These will be the hob plates, so the idea is to make them waterproof so that if any liquid is spilled on the cooker surface, it will not make the paint run.

3 You can either buy colored knobs, or paint plain knobs a nice bright color. I used untreated pine knobs so I gave them one coat of primer first, then a few coats of red enamel paint.

4 Paint your unit the desired final color and let dry. I used a water-based eggshell paint in a very pale gray and it took two coats.

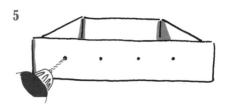

5 To attach the knobs to the front, you could glue them on using a glue gun but if you want them to be able to turn you need to drill some holes. Measure across the front and mark the equidistant points where you want to position you knobs. Drill holes at these points (see page 121). Make the hole larger than the diameter of the screw or bolt so that it can turn freely once inserted.

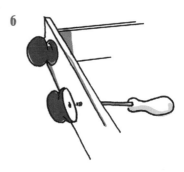

6 To attach the knobs, push the screws into the holes from the inside of the drawer (with the point sticking outward) and use a screwdriver to screw the screws into your knobs. Don't tighten fully so that they can turn a little. You could put a drop of glue on the point of the screw before screwing on the knob for extra security if you wish.

7 Stick your coaster hobs on the top, making sure they are evenly spaced (I marked the positions with masking tape). I used a glue gun but you could use any glue that will bond cork and wood. If you want your play cooker to be especially hardwearing, then give the whole thing a coat of varnish to protect it. That's it—start cooking!

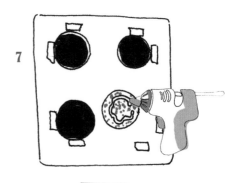

VARIATIONS

• Plastic sticky-backed hooks on the sides make a great place to hang toy utensils.

• Stick a little battery-powered, push-on light inside the cabinet as a stove light.

• Add a long horizontal handle for hanging toy dish towels or oven mitts.

• Add the stove door "glass" by cutting out a round cornered square of silver card and gluing to the front.

Louvred Art Gallery

Any object where it is obvious that a lot of skill has gone into the making of it is hard for me to abandon. These old shutters, which still function perfectly, are such an object. With a few licks of paint and a bit of imagination they have been transformed into a versatile "art gallery" display for a kid's room (or any room for that matter). Simply place your favorite picture and postcards between the slats to create an instant and flexible display.

YOU WILL NEED

Louvred shutter or small door (with slats that move)

TSP (sugar soap) solution

Old newspapers or dust sheet

White matt latex paint (emulsion)

Colored matt latex paint (emulsion)—a sample pot will be enough for one shutter

Paintbrush

Scraper

Sandpaper

Decorator's varnish, satin finish

Flat bracket (optional)

Mirror plates and wall fixings

1 Clean the shutter well and make sure it is free from dust, dirt, and grease. Use a solution of TSP or sugar soap to create a key for your paint. Rinse and let dry.

2 On a flat work surface, lay out newspapers or a dust sheet to catch any paint and then place your shutter on top, with the rods underneath—you will only paint the side that is visible. Have the slats pointing upward so that they will hold paper later on. Coat the shutter with a generous layer of white paint, taking care to avoid any drips. Paint the slats first, getting into the corners and paying special attention to the top edges of the slats, then work around the frame and sides. Let dry, then paint with two coats of colored paint.

3 To create an aged and distressed look, use a paint scraping tool or sandpaper to rub paint away along any edges that may usually be exposed to wear and tear. Start with a few areas and slowly build up until you achieve your desired effect. Use the sandpaper to soften edges, too, after you have scraped them.

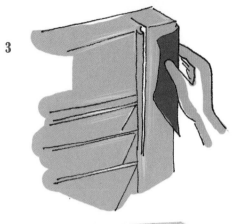

4 Remove any dust from the sanding and scraping first and then coat with a layer of decorator's varnish to seal and protect the surface. Let dry.

5 If you'd like to hang the shutter on the wall, attach mirror plates to the back (see page 83) or simply prop it up against the wall and let the floor take the weight; add mirror plates at the top screwed to the wall to stop it falling over if knocked.

VARIATIONS

• Extend the gallery by adding more shutters. Some hinge together with pins or you could use screw hinges to connect them. To keep two shutters together and stop them from folding, screw flat brackets across from one to the other on the back. Three hinged together could make a small room divider or screen.

• To achieve an aged look that suggests the shutter has been painted many times before, add a paint layer of a contrasting color instead of the white base, or even on top of it. When you scrape back, this color will be revealed.

• Add small cup hooks to the wooden frame for hanging other items or paint with magnetic chalkboard paint so you can write messages, artwork "titles," and pin things with magnets (for older children).

• Make a kitchen tidy and hang your utensils from the shutters using little butcher's hooks (s-hooks).

• You could add a magnetic strip to keep your knives tidy and accessible, too.

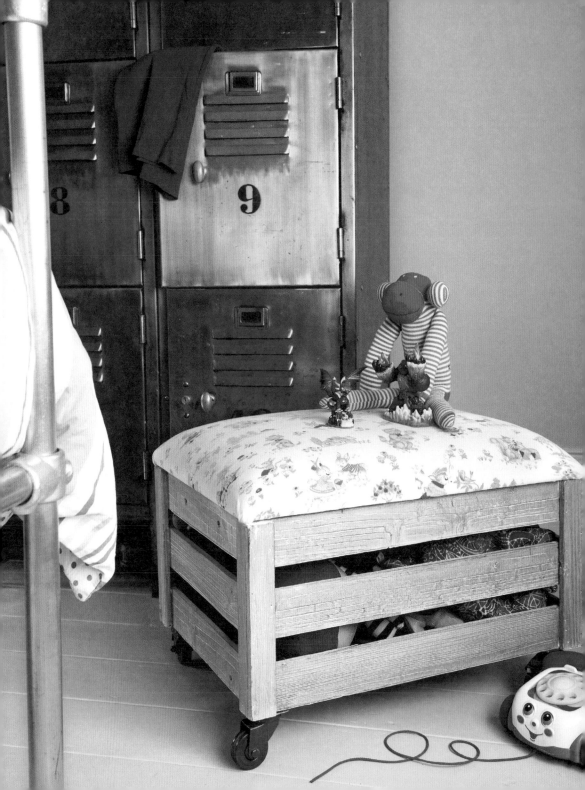

Crate Toy Storage

Old wooden crates and boxes make practical and good-looking storage solutions. This project takes the idea one step further with the addition of a padded lid, making your storage solution work as a seat, too. For real flexibility, add some lockable castors and you'll wonder how you ever managed without one!

1 Measure the top of the crate in both directions. My crate was wider at the corners than the sides, so I measured to this edge, which created an overhang on each side—perfect for lifting the lid. However, it's fine if your crate is a standard rectangle and the lid sits flush with the edge. Cut your MDF to this measurement, wearing safety goggles and working in a well-ventilated area, or get it cut for you at a lumber yard. Check the crate over and remove any rogue nails or splinters and lightly sand away any rough edges.

YOU WILL NEED

Old apple crate or other wooden box

½in (12mm) MDF, cut to size of crate top (see step 1), plus offcuts (see step 11)

Sandpaper (optional)

Foam to cover the lid, 2in (5cm) deep

All-purpose glue (optional)

Staple gun

4oz batting (wadding)

Fabric for lid, cut to size of lid plus at least 5in (12cm) extra on all sides for turning

Water-based white paint

Paintbrush

Decorator's varnish (optional)

4 lockable castors

TSP (sugar soap) solution

Sandpaper (optional)

Non-toxic spray paint (such as Plastikote)

16 x size 8 screws, ¾in (2cm) and screwdriver

Drill and small wood drill bit (size 2.5)

2

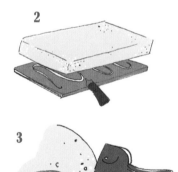

2 Cut your foam to the same size as your lid and position it centrally on the top. You can glue it in place if you wish, which will make the next step easier, but it's not essential. Apply all-purpose glue generously to the lid top, align the foam, and press down firmly. It will dry in 2–4 hours.

3

3 With the bottom edge of the foam in line with the edge of the MDF, take hold of the top edge, pull it down so that it meets the bottom edge, and staple in place (stapling into the top surface of the lid right next to the very edge). Do this all the way around the edges to create the curved shape of the padded lid.

4

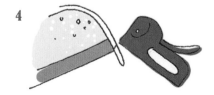

4 Next, cut your piece of batting (wadding) to the size of the top, plus at least 3in (7.5cm) all around. Lay the wadding over the foam and staple it halfway along the bottom edge on one side, into the side of the MDF.

5 Smooth the wadding over to the opposite side and again staple the bottom edge to the side of the MDF, halfway along. Repeat on the two remaining sides, making sure that you are smoothing out the wadding as you work so that it will lie nicely. Staple all the way around the edges, positioning the staples right next to each other, and then trim away the excess wadding from the edge.

6 Cut your top fabric and lining, if using, to size, allowing extra for turning. On a flat, clean surface lay your top fabric right side down with the lining fabric on top. Place the lid, padded side down, centrally over the fabric. Take hold of the fabric about halfway along one of the long sides and pull it so that it lies flat against the batting and extends onto the underside of the lid. Fold the edge back under itself for neatness and add a staple.

7 Repeat on the other long side, gently pulling so that there is a little tension in the fabric (but not too much to distort the padded shape) and then on the two short sides. Turn the lid over; does the tension look even? If so, continue stapling along all the edges until the fabric is secure. If not, remove the staples and try again until you are happy. Make the line of staples as neat as possible. For the corners, cut away any excess just leaving a flap from the corner, pull over, and staple down (see also page 82).

8 Mix one part white water-based paint with three parts water to create your whitewash. Using a large paintbrush, give the crate a coat of whitewash and let dry. For a whiter looking crate, you can either reduce the amount of water in the whitewash mixture, such as two parts water to one part paint, or build up layers of whitewash. I wanted the wood to show through so used 2 coats of a thin wash. For protection, finish with a layer of clear varnish.

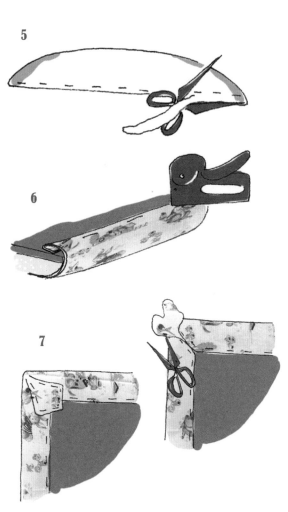

5

6

7

Tip
I used a vintage piece of French children's fabric from the 1940s for my lid and while it was fairly sturdy, I thought it best to support the fabric by lining it with white cotton underneath.

9 De-grease the castors by cleaning with TSP (sugar soap) solution and washing down with a clean cloth and drying thoroughly. You can lightly sand the metal if you want to create a firmer key for your paint. In a well-ventilated area, spray the castors all over with a non-toxic spray paint and let dry. I chose a bright red for a pop of color and to complement the red in my fabric.

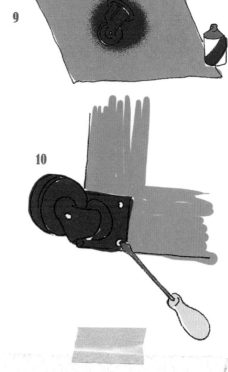

10 Turn your crate upside down and position your castors one at each corner. Mark on the wood where the holes are in the plates for the screws to go. Remove the castors and drill small pilot holes into these marks using a small drill bit for wood (see page 121). Reposition the castors and using your screwdriver, drive in four screws per castor (one in each corner).

11 If the base of your crate is thin, cut four pieces of wood or MDF the same size or slightly larger than the plates of your castors and at least ½in (1cm) thick. When screwing on the castors, place this wood inside the crate in the corners to give the screws extra wood to bite into and strengthen their hold.

VARIATIONS

• Add beading under the lid to keep it in place. To do this, measure the crate from inside wall to inside wall. Mark these measurements on the base of your lid in pencil to show where the outer edge of your beading will sit. Make another mark ½in (1cm) in toward the center and when you are stapling the fabric over, staple along this line. Cut the beading to size (miter the corners if you wish), line it up over your rows of staples, and fix to the lid using panel pins and a hammer. Now your lid will stay in place and you've also covered up all those staples too!

• Use oilcloth on the lid for a wipeable, kid-proof surface.

• Bolt two crates side by side for a toy storage bench with one long lid.

• Line the crate with fabric as you would a linen basket.

• Swap the kid's fabric for something more elegant and transfer it to the living room to house your favorite magazines or use as a side table or extra seat.

• Drill two holes in each side where you'd like a handle to go and thread colored rope (to match the castors) through the holes. Tie off in knots on the inside of the crate.

Découpage Suitcase

Vintage suitcases come in all shapes and colors. In the 1970s, when Mr Bernard Sadow had the brilliant idea of adding wheels to luggage, these old cases were somewhat sidelined but they still function perfectly well for extra storage in the home. Here, they've been decorated with a découpage design of vintage paper doll clothes and accessories, which can also serve to remind you what you're keeping inside!

Tip
To remove a musty odor from inside the case, spray with a 50/50 mixture of cool water and white vinegar. Do not soak. Leave open to dry. Repeat as necessary. Finish with a spray of air freshener if you wish or leave a used tumble drier fragranced sheet inside.

YOU WILL NEED

Vintage suitcase or hat case

TSP (sugar soap) solution

Paper doll clothes and/or accessories

Paintbrushes

PVA glue

Varnish, use a clear, water-based decorator's varnish for use in a child's room

Plastic spatula (optional)

Water, white vinegar, spray bottle (optional)

1 Clean the suitcase exterior thoroughly, rinse off, and let dry. TSP or sugar soap solution is great for cleaning away any residual dirt, grease, and even tobacco residue. For vinyl cases, you could use a car upholstery cleaning product.

2 Lay out your paper dolls clothes. I chose hat designs for my hat case and little outfits for my suitcase. Experiment by placing them on your case to see what works. Take a digital photo of your final arrangement if you want, for visual reference.

2

3 Use a brush or plastic spatula to apply a layer of glue to the back of one paper piece, taking care to go right to the edges, and then position it on your case. Push down all over to make sure it is stuck down well. Repeat with the other paper pieces until you have covered the area you're working on. Use your photo to help you remember what goes where.

4 As the paper dries, check for any edges that curl up and re-apply glue to stick them down again. I found that "clothes" cut from card rather than paper curled up more, so be generous with the glue and, if necessary, lay something heavy on top (that you don't mind getting glue onto) so that they dry flat. Once dry, check again that all the papers have glued down completely and re-apply glue as required.

3

5 Using a small paintbrush, apply a layer of clear varnish over the whole area that you have découpaged. If your suitcase has piping round the edge, wipe round this with paper towel to remove any stray varnish. If you see small air bubbles forming in the varnish, gently brush over them to remove. Let dry.

5

6 Apply one or two more layers of varnish until you have created a sealed surface. Wait for each layer to dry before applying the next. Your case is now ready for a new lease of life!

Toy Bookends

Old wooden toy cars and vehicles ooze timeless vintage style and can evoke a strong sense of nostalgia for the toys we played with in our own childhoods. Use larger wooden toys that have been broken, are no longer loved, or just crying out for a revamp and reinvent them as a pair of bookends to bring a stylish touch to your storage solutions.

YOU WILL NEED

Large wooden toy car

Saw

MDF, about 1in (2.5cm) thick, cut to size (see step 2)

Drill, wood drill bits, countersink

6 x wood screws, 1¼in (3cm) long

Screwdriver

Hot glue gun or all-purpose glue

MDF sealant and brush

Primer (optional)

Enamel spray paint in chrome finish

Self-adhesive felt

1 Measure the length of the car and mark the mid-point at a natural break. If the mid-point will dissect an important feature, like the windshield, then move your cutting line along to avoid it. Try to keep the pieces as even as possible. If you will cut through the steering wheel, for example, then put it to one side to be glued back into place later. Cut the car in half using a hand saw, cutting as straight a line as possible.

2 Measure out the MDF for the bookends. The width of the base should be at least the width of your car and the length should be at least the length of the longest car section plus an extra 1in (2.5cm) to allow room for the thickness of the bookend upright. Wear safety goggles and work in a well-ventilated space to cut two pieces this size, or get the MDF cut at a lumber yard.

3

3 Now take the measurement for the bookend uprights. Make them the same width as the bookend bases. Stand the upright in position on top of the base end and mark the desired height. Cut two pieces this size. For holding larger books you can make the uprights taller or for smaller books you can keep them short. Ideally they should be taller than the tallest point on your car.

4

4 Take one bookend base and turn it upside down. At one short end drill three evenly spaced pilot holes ½in (1cm) in from the edge. Now countersink these holes so that your screw heads can lie flat. Repeat on the other base.

5 Put some old books or blocks of wood on your work surface to the height of the upright, so the flat base can connect with the bottom of the upright. Your bookend is positioned upside down at this point and you are working from the underside. Put the wood screws into the holes, line up the MDF pieces, and screw them together. Repeat to make the other bookend.

6 Position the car sections. You may need to put a spot of glue between the wheels and the car body to stop them turning. Glue down any other moving parts that you want to secure. Use some scrap wood or similar to pack underneath your car to support it and keep it level, and once in position glue it into place on the upright. Let dry. Repeat with the other car section and bookend base. If using all-purpose glue that takes longer to set, you can glue the wheels to the base too for extra strength.

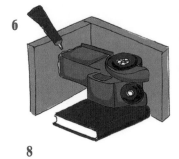

7 Brush on a coat of MDF sealant to prepare the bookends for painting. Apply sealant to the car, too, if it has not been sealed by varnish or paint already. Paint both bookends with a primer (if required).

8 Working in a well-ventilated area, spray the bookends and car all over with a chrome finish spray paint. Spray lightly and often rather than one heavy coat, to avoid drips. Pay special attention to edges, interiors, and fiddly bits! If you have a steering wheel or similar that you had to cut off earlier, spray paint that too. Once dry, use the hot glue gun to glue it into position on the bookend upright.

9 Cut two pieces of adhesive felt to the same size as the base. Peel away the backing paper and, starting from one short end, gently apply, smoothing out as you go. If the felt stretches slightly or wasn't cut accurately you can trim off any excess along the edges afterward with sharp scissors.

VARIATIONS

• Instead of cutting a large toy in half, you can upcycle pairs of smaller toys instead. Make the bookends as described above and glue one toy to each bookend before painting. Pairs of dinosaurs, horses, or other plastic figurines work well.

• Use ornaments or china figurines instead of toys, anything that might look good as a pair and spray the bookends with a bronze spray paint for a more grown-up, antique-looking effect.

Tea Card Mini Bunting

Tea cards were mass-produced in the 1950s and 60s and were given away with various brands of tea. Designed to be educational, they have all sorts of wonderful designs and illustrations on them from birds, animals, plants, and flowers to cars and flags of the world. Still traded today, you can often pick them up at garage sales for very little and with such beautiful vintage illustrations they are perfect for turning into decorative mini-bunting or even gift tags.

Tip
Using wide ribbon and then folding it over makes it nice and thick so that the cards stay in position. It's fine to use thin ribbon, but to stop the cards slipping, tie a knot in the ribbon behind each card as you work. To space them accurately, measure as you go.

YOU WILL NEED

Vintage tea cards (approx 10 per yard/meter of ribbon)

Single hole punch

Ribbon, about ¾in (2cm) wide x length of your bunting

Sewing machine and thread

Measuring tape or ruler (optional)

1 Lay out your tea cards. Select the ones that are portrait format (so that they can hang downward) and lay them out in the order you'd like them to hang. Grouping cards by theme works well. Mix up the colors and subjects for an even spread of designs.

2 Using the single hole punch, carefully punch a hole just in from each top corner. Don't punch too near the edge as the cards may rip when threaded.

2

3 Fold the ribbon into three lengthwise (see tip on page 111). Either pin to hold the fold in place or fold it as you feed it into the sewing machine. Sew down the ribbon, using a zigzag stitch in a contrasting color for decoration or a straight stitch in a matching color thread. Using scissors, cut across the ends of the ribbon at a 45-degree angle to create a sharp point for threading.

4 Select the card from the middle of your spread and start to thread the ribbon through it. Push the ribbon from front to back on the right-hand side, pull through some excess, and then thread the ribbon from back to front through the left hole. The ribbon should run between the holes across the back of the card leaving the design on the front clearly visible. You may need to twist the ribbon so that it is lying flat at the back. Have the "flat" side of the ribbon facing forward and the fold facing the back.

5 Move this middle card along the ribbon so that it is centrally placed. Now thread the left side of the ribbon with the cards from the left of your spread. Repeat with the right side. Once threaded, check they are evenly spaced and adjust if necessary. You can do this by eye or use a tape measure or ruler for more accuracy. Now they're ready to hang up!

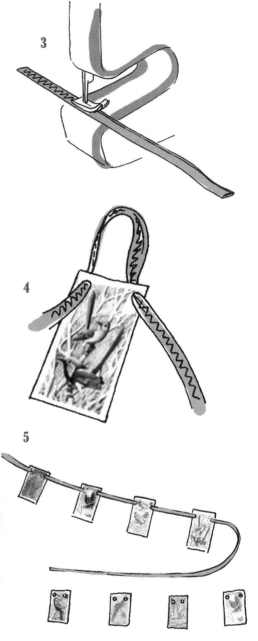

VARIATIONS

• Make gift tags: glue plain card or paper to the back of the tea card and trim off any excess. Punch a hole through the top center, thread onto some ribbon or string, and write your message on the reverse.

• Use bias binding to hold the cards. Sew along the binding and insert the top of a card at even intervals to sew through, too.

Russian Doll Light Pull

Russian dolls—"Matryoshka"—are always a great vintage find with their bright and cheerful folk patterns and sweet hand-painted faces. They're often discarded because one of the original line-up was damaged or lost, but you don't need a full set to make a gorgeous light pull, just three dolls in ascending size can be transformed into this beautiful and original handle.

YOU WILL NEED

3 Russian dolls, 3½in, 2½in, and 1½in (9cm, 6cm, and 4cm) tall

Drill and wood drill bits, size 2.5 and 4

Ribbon

All-purpose glue, wood glue, or hot glue gun

Scissors

1 Separate each of the Russian dolls and set aside the base of the largest doll. Using the smaller drill bit (size 2.5), drill through the center of the tops of the heads of all the dolls and the middle of the bases of the medium and small dolls. Then replace the drill bit with the larger bit (size 4) and drill through the same holes again, to enlarge them. Brush away any wood shavings.

2 Take one end of the ribbon and wrap it round something hard and thin. The smaller drill bit is perfect for this but a match or a tapestry needle would also work.

3 Push the wrapped ribbon down through the top of the head of the smallest doll until it is threaded on. Then push it through the base of the smallest doll, through the inside of the base. Now you should be able to assemble this doll with the ribbon running through it from top to bottom. Repeat with the medium-sized doll.

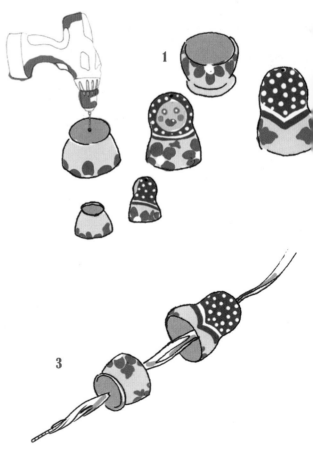

4 Thread the ribbon through the top of the head of the largest doll and knot the end several times until you create a large knot that will not slip through the drilled hole. Holding the doll's head, pull the ribbon taut from the top to check that it holds in place. Trim off any excess ribbon if necessary.

5 Apply glue just inside where the dolls meet in the middle—their "waist" area—and push shut. Let dry. If you want them all to face the same way, align them and add a drop of glue where the head of one meets the base of the one above, making sure you've pulled the ribbon tight first to avoid getting glue on the ribbon if it's not in the right position. To add weight to the handle, insert something heavy, such as washers and nuts, curtain weights, or fishing weights, inside the largest doll before gluing shut.

6 To hang, tie the top of the ribbon onto the existing cord of your light fitting and trim to size.

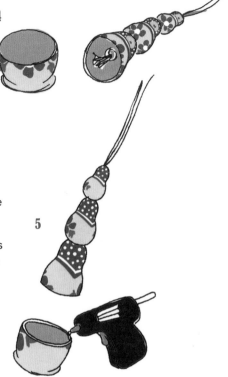

VARIATIONS

• Add colorful beads between each doll.

• Use cord instead of ribbon or create double-sided ribbon by folding it over before threading. You could run a line of stitches along the center of the ribbon to keep it together.

• Try this with other items; anything you can easily drill through and thread ribbon through (or tie onto)—little yellow rubber ducks would make a fun light pull for a bathroom!

Hula Hoop Hideout

Kids love playing peek-a-boo and creating little dens to hide in. This project shows you how to make a simple children's hideout using a vintage curtain, a hula hoop, and inexpensive voile or net curtains, that can even be converted into a bed canopy! It also packs down to nearly nothing for when playtime is over.

YOU WILL NEED

2 x tab-top voile curtains

1 x long vintage curtain (or fabric)

1 x hula hoop

Sewing machine, needle, and thread

Craft knife and gaffer (duct) tape (optional)

Ribbon, rope, or cord for hanging

1 Wash and press your tab-top curtains. Remove any curtain tape from the top of your vintage curtain, wash, and press. Place the tab-top curtains together, right sides facing, and pin and sew along one long edge to make one large curtain.

2 Fold the vintage curtain in half widthwise to find the center, then cut it in half along the crease from top to bottom so that you end up with two long strips.

3 Lay out the tab-top curtain with right side facing. Select the vintage strip with the freshly cut raw edge on the right-hand edge. Place this on top of the left-hand side of the large curtain, right side up and left edges aligned, 23½in (60cm) down from the top hem of the curtain; pin. Baste (tack) the top of the vintage strip to the curtain. Stop basting ¼in (5mm) from the end. Turn under ¼in (5mm) on the raw, right-hand edge of the vintage strip hem and pin then topstitch in place. Continue along the bottom edge and the left-hand side, or you can leave these edges unattached if you wish.

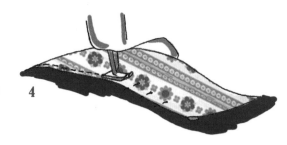

4 Repeat with the other vintage strip on the right-hand side, again 23½in (60cm) down from the tab top hem and with the right edges aligned. Pin along those edges. Baste (tack) the top of the vintage strip, turn back a ¼in (5mm) seam and pin. Topstitch the sides and bottom edge as before.

5 Lay the curtain out flat again, right side up. Fold down the tab-top edge toward you so that the fold is on the 23½in (60cm) line you measured before. Use the top of the vintage strips to guide you, too. Pin in place. Measure down 2in (5cm) from the fold for the hula hoop channel and sew along this line right across the curtain. Remove all the pins.

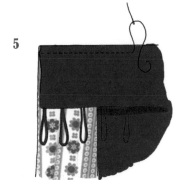

6 Find the join in your hula hoop and gently pull it apart. Thread one end of the hula hoop through the channel until all of the curtain has been threaded on and the end reappears. Now re-close your hula hoop over the inner tube. If you have a different type of hula hoop or can't find the join, then carefully cut through it with a sturdy craft knife and use gaffer (duct) tape to rejoin it.

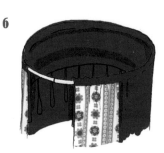

7 Gather all your tabs together and thread through some ribbon, rope, or a long strip of fabric for hanging. Hang up in your desired location. Check the drop and if you want to, trim off any excess fabric from the bottom and hem.

VARIATIONS

• Sew a buttonhole on each side seam for threading tie backs through.

• Make a bed canopy: omit step 2 and work on the tab-top curtains separately, or even add more panels so that they can drape out over a larger area. Keep the fabrics light and floaty to avoid adding too much weight to the hoop.

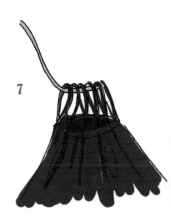

Workshop Techniques

For some of the projects you will need to use some basic workshop techniques to drill holes into and cut through various materials. I've also included a brief guide to fixing your creations safely to the wall.

Drilling Metal

Drilling through metal may seem quite daunting but it's a straightforward and simple process with the right tools for the job.

1 Secure the metal and mark your position. Clamp the metal you wish to drill to a workstation or hold it in a vice to make it secure. Use a pencil and ruler to precisely mark where you want to drill. Then hold a nail to your mark and drive it in slightly with a hammer to create a dent. Use this dent to position your drill bit for an accurate start to your drilling.

2 Select the correct drill bit and set the drill into position. Line the drill bit up with the dent. Make sure it's level (some drills have integrated leveling bubbles to help). Apply a steady pressure. For hard metals, drill slowly and steadily. For softer metals, drill faster (too slow and the metal shavings may melt) but never higher than a medium speed.

3 Remove the drill bit as soon as you have reached the desired depth. Keep the bit spinning until you have removed it entirely from the metal.

DRILL BITS

FOR DRILLING METAL: HSS (High Speed Steel) drill bits are designed to work on most types of metals, as are carbon steel bits that are coated with titanium nitride (TiN). For hard metals, such as stainless steel (see the Tea Tray Magnetic Board, page 50), you can also use a cobalt steel bit.

FOR DRILLING WOOD: "Brad Point" bits (or "Lip and Spur" bits) are recommended for drilling holes in wood up to ½in (12mm). These drill bits are identifiable by having a pointy end (rather than a round one). For larger holes, use a flat wood bit (which looks like a very large flat head screwdriver tip with a sharp spike).

COUNTERSINK: A countersink drill bit cuts a conical hole that allows your screw to sit flush with the surface.

SCREWDRIVER BIT: A drill bit with a screwdriver head makes short work of screwing in screws.

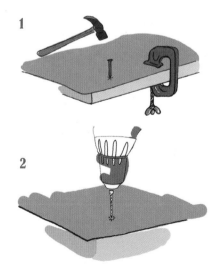

1

2

Drilling Wood

Unleash your inner carpenter with this guide to drilling into wood to fix screws or to join pieces together.

1 Secure the wood and mark your position. Clamp the wood you wish to drill to a workstation or hold it in a vice to make it secure. Use a pencil and ruler to precisely mark where you want to drill.

2 Select the correct drill bit. Line the drill bit up with the mark and gently press the pointed end of the bit in the center of your mark and twist slightly. Make sure it's level (some drills have integrated leveling bubbles to help you).

3 Drill slowly and surely. Wood is best drilled at a slow and steady speed. Drill too fast and you risk the wood splintering or even burning. A good tip to avoid splintering is to drill your hole until the tip begins to appear through the other side, remove the bit, and then drill in from the reverse side.

4 Remove the drill bit as soon as you have reached the desired depth. Keep the bit spinning until you have removed it entirely from the wood to avoid it sticking.

> **Tip**
> To avoid drilling into your work surface, place a flat piece of scrap wood underneath.

Quick Guide to Wood Types

Some projects require the addition of new wooden elements and you will need to source from a lumber yard or home improvement store. Here's a brief guide to the different types:

MDF (MEDIUM-DENSITY FIBERBOARD)

Made by combining wood fibers with a wax or resin binder and applying high temperature and pressure to produce panels. Releases dust particles when cut so must be worked on in a very well-ventilated area, preferably wearing a respirator or dust mask. Sealant recommended.

SOFTWOOD

Wood from evergreen trees. Opt for sustainably grown softwoods (grown on tree farms to ensure an endless supply of wood and relatively easy to find) to avoid contributing to deforestation.

PLYWOOD

Made by layering thin sheets of wood veneer at right angles to each other and gluing to create a composite material. Very strong, reusable, and can usually be manufactured locally.

Fixing to Walls

The first thing to do when fixing something to a wall is to determine what kind of wall it is. A solid wall (made of masonry, block work, or concrete and perhaps plastered over) or a hollow wall (plasterboards attached to studs, for example), will each require a separate kind of fixing.

Safety first

Always check your walls first for hidden pipes or electrical cables before attempting to drill. There are pipe and cable detectors available from home improvement stores that can check this. Use safety goggles when operating power tools.

FIXING TO SOLID WALLS

1 Mark the wall. Mark the position of the item and mark the fixing points in pencil. Once marked, remove the item and put to one side.

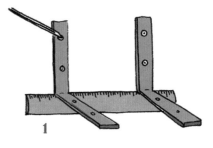

2 Select your masonry bit. Check the rawl plug package for instructions on which size drill bit to use and which size screws, and follow these recommendations.

3 Mark the depth on the drill bit. To ensure the plug sits flush in the hole, hold the plug level with the end of the bit and use masking tape wrapped around the bit to mark out the length of the plug.

4 Drill. Place the drill bit on your mark and start to drill slowly; you can speed up when it has begun to cut into the surface. Don't go too fast as a moderate speed is more effective. Drill until you reach the depth you need, using the masking tape to guide you. Once the edge of the tape reaches the wall then you have drilled the required depth. Remove the drill bit carefully from the wall.

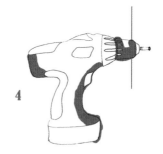

5 Insert the plug and fix the screws. Place the rawl plug into the hole and give a light tap with a hammer to drive it home. It should be a tight fit. Put your item to be hung into position and place a screw through it and align it with the center of the plug hole. The screw needs to be long enough to go through the item and along the full length of the plug (no longer). Begin to tighten the screw. The plug will expand and grip the sides of the hole giving you a good fix. Continue until the item is secured.

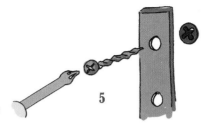

FIXING TO HOLLOW WALLS

Find the studs that the plasterboards are fixed to and use those to drill and fix into.

1 Locate the timbers. To find the studs in the wall you can use a stud finder tool. Alternatively, knock on the wall until the hollow sound changes to a muffled sound. This is probably a stud. If you have difficulty finding a stud, or they are not in convenient places, you will have to fix into the plasterboard itself, although this is not suitable for heavy items and will require special "hollow wall" rawl plugs.

2 Mark your fixing points. Hold up your item to be fixed and mark where you wish to drill your hole. Make it align with the stud where the wall sounds solid.

3 Drill into your marks. Use a small diameter drill bit to drill into your marks. If you find yourself drilling into wood then you have correctly identified the stud positions!

4 Fix your item. Position your item and use screws to drill straight into the wooden studs to secure.

Sewing Techniques

You don't need to be a proficient seamstress to create any of the stitched projects, and most can be sewn by hand. However, a sewing machine will speed things along if you have one. I have included a brief guide to sewing basic seams and hems, and a few hand stitches for finishing touches, which should get you under way in recreating beautiful projects from all those fabulous vintage fabrics.

PREPARING FABRICS

Before sewing your fabrics always launder them and press them well to remove any creases. Vintage fabrics should be carefully hand-washed in warm or cold water. Take special care with silk or delicate items, considering whether they need laundering at all or whether dry-cleaning would be a safer option. To brighten yellowed lace or doilies, fill a saucepan with water, drop in some slices of lemon, and bring to a boil. Remove from the heat, add your doilies,

and leave for an hour until the water cools. You can let dry in the sun too, as sunlight helps the whitening process.

To remove musty smells, use white vinegar or lemon juice mixed with warm water (1:1) and spray the affected area. Musty smells are caused by mold and the acidity of the vinegar (or lemons) will combat this. Wash in soapy water afterward, if possible.

Seams

You create a seam when you stitch two or more pieces of fabric together.

PINNING AND BASTING

Before you sew a seam, pin the layers of fabric together with right sides facing and match the raw edges. Place the pins at right angles to the edge. You can also baste (tack) them together by hand to prevent them slipping. Thread a needle with a long piece of thread in a contrast color and take evenly spaced stitches through both layers, stitching close to the seam line and within the seam allowance. You can take several stitches onto your needle at one time, before drawing the thread through the fabric. You will remove the basting thread once the seam is stitched.

STRAIGHT SEAM

1 Pin and baste (tack), if you like, your two fabrics together with their right sides facing and raw edges aligned.

2 Position the fabric pieces under the machine foot, lining the edges with the correct seam guideline. Position the needle about ½in (12mm) down on the seam line and lower the presser foot. Set your machine to reverse and stitch backward, almost to the top edge. Change the setting to stitch forward, and stitch down the seam line.

3 Reverse stitch at the end of your seam again to secure the thread. Cut the threads close to the stitching.

4 To stitch a corner, continue to stitch until you reach about ½in (12mm) from the end of your seam (or the specified seam allowance). Stop stitching with the needle down in the fabric. Raise the presser foot, pivot the fabric through 90 degrees, lower the foot, and continue to stitch to the end of the seam.

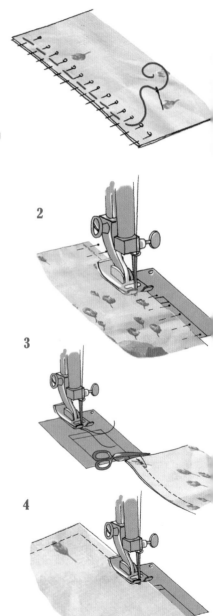

2

3

4

FINISHING SEAMS

Always press your seams to give a neat finish. Press the seam open so that the seam allowance lies flat. If you have several layers of fabric, trim the seam allowance close to the stitched edge.

Finish seams on fabrics that fray easily by zigzag stitching the raw edges, or using an overlocker if your machine has one. To get a neat point on corners, cut across the corner of the seam turnings, close to the stitching but taking care not to cut through the actual stitches.

A SIMPLE HEM

You can finish the raw edge of your fabric with a simple hem.

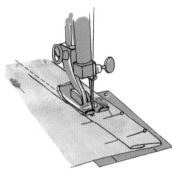

Turn up the depth of the hem, press, and pin in place. Machine stitch close to the raw edge. For a neater edge, fold a double hem by turning up ½in (12mm), pressing the fold, and then folding again by about 1in (2.5cm), or the depth of your hem. Press the fold. Machine stitch close to the first folded edge.

Hand stitches

These are both practical and add a decorative finishing touch.

SLIP STITCH

This is used to finish a seam or close gaps in a seam (in a pillow cover, for example), from the right side of the fabric.

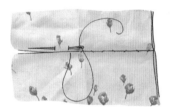

Secure the thread and, working from right to left, bring the needle through one folded edge, slip the needle through the fold of the opposite edge for about ¼in (5mm), and draw the needle and thread through. Continue catching both folds to join the edges.

OVERCAST OR WHIP STITCH

This can be used to join two fabrics, for example the edges of the tapestries in the Tapestry Footstool project on page 13.

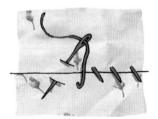

Secure the thread and take diagonal stitches over the edge of each seam allowance, about ¼in (5mm) apart.

BACKSTITCH

This is a strong stitch that looks a little like machine stitching.

Secure the thread and, working from right to left, bring the needle to the front a stitch length along from the start of the stitching. Insert the needle back a stitch length and then bring it up a stitch length in front of where it first came up. Insert the needle back a stitch length and continue working back and forth along the line.

Sourcing Vintage Items

When sourcing vintage items it's best to go with your mind open to the possibilities of what you might find. If sourcing for specific projects, it can help to make a list of what you are looking for, as it's very easy to get distracted! Personally, my best ideas started with finding an object that intrigued me and had something about it that made me want to own it.

WHERE TO LOOK

Garage and yard sales, and vintage fairs
These often start early in the morning, so wear comfy shoes, dress for the weather, and have a good breakfast to keep your strength up. Get stuck in early and have a good rummage around. Don't be afraid to haggle—it can be fun!

Thrift stores
These can often yield fantastic results and normally have a quick turnover of stock, so make a habit of regularly visiting your local stores.

Friends and family
If you're looking for specific items, try asking friends and family for help or information. You never know, the item you're searching for might be the very thing your aunty has been meaning to throw away for ages.

Online auctions or market places
Online research can sometimes prove fruitful but stick to a budget as auction prices can escalate quickly if you get caught up in the excitement of bidding.

Classified adverts
Check your local papers or notices in general stores, especially for larger items such as furniture, and check your local recycling plant or network for items others no longer want but don't want to send to landfill. You might just discover a vintage gem!

Resources

Ellie Laycock (author)
www.huntedandstuffed.com
Twitter: @huntednstuffed
Owner of Hunted and Stuffed: beautiful luxury homeware made with upcycled vintage textiles.
Ships worldwide.

Materials
Borovick Fabrics Ltd. (UK)
16 Berwick Street
London, W1F 0HP
020 7437 2180
www.borovickfabricsltd.co.uk
Third generation family-run fabric business in the heart of Soho.

Fulham Timber Merchants Ltd. (UK)
Brixton Branch, Unit 9, Ellerslie Square Industrial Estate,
Lyham Road, London, SW2 5DZ
020 7738 3268
www.fulhamtimber.co.uk
Helpful timber merchants and hardware suppliers.

Hobbycraft (UK)
www.hobbycraft.co.uk
Stores nationwide.

Hobby Lobby (US)
www.hobbylobby.com
Stores nationwide.

John Lewis (UK)
www.johnlewis.com
Stores nationwide.

Lowe's (US)
www.lowes.com
General hardware supplies.

Michael's (US/Canada)
www.michaels.com
Stores nationwide.

Rachel Goodchild Designs (UK)
Studio 26, 42 Triangle West,
Park Street, Clifton, Bristol, BS8 1ES
www.rachelgoodchild.com
Beautiful gift wrap designs: Rachel designed the paper used in the Crate Bedside Table project.

Simply Fabrics (UK)
48 Atlantic Road
London, SW9 8JN
020 7733 2877
Best fabric shop in South London. Robert stocks great factory remnants too.

Upcycling and recycling
Creatively Recycling
www.creativelyrecycling.com
A blog by Rachel Goodchild (see above).

Hipcycle (US)
www.hipcycle.com
Online store with upcycled goods—ships to the US and Canada.

The Old Cinema (UK)
160 Chiswick High Road
London, W14 1PR
www.theoldcinema.co.uk
Pioneering champions of upcycling in the UK, Martin and co. fill this converted cinema with gorgeous vintage, industrial, and upcycled gems.

Upcycled (UK)
www.upcycled.co.uk
An upcycling hub website run by The Old Cinema.

Upcycle Magazine
www.upcyclemagazine.com
Project ideas, product reviews, and stories from the world of upcycling, recycling, and reusing.

SOURCING VINTAGE

Brixi (UK)
Unit 7, Brixton Village,
London, SW9 8PR
07919 162 428
Fabulous Aladdin's cave of vintage, upcycled, and modern pieces.
Car Boot Sales (UK and EU)
www.carbootsales.org
Search for local sales near you.

The Freecycle Network (worldwide)
www.freecycle.org
Freecycling is an international movement where a person passes on, for free, an unwanted item to another person who needs that item. Find a group near you in participating countries, including the US and UK, via the website.

GreenFlea (US)
www.greenfleamarkets.com
A large indoor and outdoor market in Manhattan in New York.

Hell's Kitchen Flea Market (US)
www.hellskitchenfleamarket.com
Three outdoor urban flea markets in New York.

Loose's Antique Emporium (UK)
www.loosesemporium.co.uk/
23-25 Magdalen Street,
Norwich, Norfolk, NR3 1LP
01603 665 600
Formerly a department store, this place is now filled with vintage furniture, textiles, and curiosities.

The Original Round Top Antiques Fair
www.roundtoptexasantiques.com
Holds four shows a year, based in Texas between Austin and Houston.

Preloved (UK)
www.preloved.co.uk
Second-hand items.

Index

Acknowledgments

I'd like to thank Claire Richardson for the beautiful photography (as always), Nel Haynes for the scrumptious styling, and Harriet de Winton for the lovely illustration, as well as my wonderful editor Katie Hardwicke and designer Vicky Rankin; plus, enormous thanks to Cindy, Sally, Penny, Carmel, and Fahema at CICO. I'd also like to thank JP for the encouragement and Yvonne for the support.